Stop – Breathe – Focus REALLY WORKS!   –Mike

Stop – Breathe – Focus saved my life!   –Jim

Stop – Breathe – Focus gave me the tools I needed to make
the right choices in my life and to understand what was really going on within me.   –Deb

Stop – Breathe – Focus helps me control myself and stay out
of trouble.   –Adam

Stop – Breathe – Focus is a very valuable tool. I particularly
got a lot out of the breathwork.   –Susie

Stop – Breathe - Focus on the problem at hand, make options,
don't just shoot off and be sorry at the end. Keep a positive
attitude even in the worst cases. This is what I learned from
the *Stop – Breathe – Focus.*   –Aaron

Thank-you! Thank-you! Thank-you! For giving me the *Stop
– Breathe – Focus!*   –Tim

Stop–Breathe–Focus

Your Key to Personal Freedom
Through Self-Management

by
Mary V. Augustyn, M.S.

Published by InnerQuest
Copyright © 2008 Mary V. Augustyn

ISBN: 978-0-9802090-1-3
Project Development: *Open Window Creations*
Cover and Book Design: *Greystroke Creative Works*
Printed in the United States of America
Cover photo by Mary V. Augustyn

Copies may be ordered from:
www.StopBreatheFocus.com

Mary V. Augustyn, M.S.
P.O. Box 2590
Breckenridge, Colorado
mary@stopbreathefocus.com

The names used in this book have been changed to
respect the anonymity of those mentioned.

Dedicated to:

Larry, my husband and partner, for his love, patience and encouragement.

Amy and Matt Palcso, my beloved daughter and son-in-law.

All of my family and friends.

Connie Moser, Elizabeth Hattab, and Betty Bissmeyer, my colleagues and friends who have so enriched my life and to our women's group that lifted me up.

All of my clients who inspired me to create the *Stop – Breathe – Focus* for them, and for their courage and strength in utilizing this tool.

Sam Mayhall, my friend and mentor—You guided me with love and faith.

And in loving memory of my parents, Valerie and Ted Federickson, who gave me the gumption to follow through on my dreams.

Reiki Ideals

Just for today I let go of anger
Just for today I let go of worry
Just for today I let go of judgment
Just for today I give thanks for my many blessings
Just for today I am honest
Just for today I am kind to my neighbor and every living thing

Adaptation by Mary V. Augustyn

I am a channel of your peace
Where there is hatred I bring love
Where there is injury your pardon, love
And where there's doubt true faith in you
I am a channel of your peace
Where there's despair in life, I bring hope
Where there is darkness, only light
And where there's sadness ever joy.
Oh, love, I grant that I may never seek,
So much to be consoled as to console
To be understood as to understand
To be loved as to love with all my soul
I am a channel of your peace
It is in pardoning that we are pardoned
In giving of ourselves that we receive
In dying that we're born to eternal life

Adaptation by Mary V. Augustyn

TABLE OF CONTENTS

TABLE OF CONTENTS – Cont.

EXERCISES:

INTRODUCTION

Stop – Breathe – Focus is a technique I originally developed to help domestic violence offenders diffuse volatile situations. I have been teaching this technique for more than a decade. Throughout these years, with hundreds of clients and trial situations, *Stop – Breathe – Focus* has proven to be effective for not only inhibiting violent behavior, but for eliminating any addictive or compulsive behavior; dealing with depression and anxiety in a positive manner; helping couples manage conflict and enhance their relationships; creating people's awareness of themselves, their wants, needs and choices; building self-esteem; and creating solutions for a myriad of problems.

I am an avid student of human nature and have always been interested in what makes people tick. Some of my life's goals are to eradicate violence, promote equality, help people realize their personal worth and take control of their lives. Observing what people do in a variety of situations, figuring out *why* people do what they do, and building a strategy for change led me to develop *Stop – Breathe – Focus* and expand it into a book. I believe in this technique and its capacity to help people take charge of their lives.

This book can help people change their lives for the better and, in some cases, even save their lives. Ours is a violent and addictive society. *Stop – Breathe – Focus* is a simple and effective technique that can interrupt dangerous and problematic behavior immediately (I am aware of two murders prevented by *Stop – Breathe – Focus*.) Or it can be used at a later time to autopsy behavior, provide insight, offer options for future situations and create a solid relapse prevention plan.

12 years ago I began working with domestic violence offenders. At that time my program was 26 weeks long. Most of the offenders in my program were back at home with their families where the

violence occurred. It became clear that they needed a way to prevent a recurrence and they needed it immediately. My technique utilizes many different approaches in one tidy, easy to use package. As more entered group and progressed through the program, they repeatedly told me how effective the tool was for self-control and how they were using it for all kinds of behavior, including alcohol and drug abuse.

My practice has many different types of clients with problems ranging from depression and anxiety to addictions, impulse disorders, relationship problems and situational difficulties. I began teaching *Stop – Breathe – Focus* to most of my clients and the results were phenomenal. Many of them began reporting that for the first time they felt as though they were truly in charge of their lives, were fully aware of every aspect of themselves, could identify thoughts and beliefs that caused problems, developed an ability to look at options, realize consequences of the options change thoughts and beliefs positively, and become fully responsible and accountable for themselves and their behavior.

Stop – Breathe – Focus has wide appeal to many types of people. Those who will be helped by this book are people with the following problems:

- Alcohol
- Anger
- Anorexia – starvation
- Bulimia - bingeing / purging
- Overeating
- Anxiety
- Attention Deficit Disorder
- Compulsive / addictive behaviors of any kind
- Depression

- Drugs
- Eating Disorders
- Gambling
- Kleptomania
- Nicotine addiction (chewing and smoking)
- Panic Attacks
- Relationship Problems
- Sexual Addiction
- Spending/Debt
- Violence toward self/others

Others who will find the book helpful are those who work with people and their problems. This can include but are not limited to:

- Addiction Treatment Providers
- Caseworkers
- Community Mental Health Agencies
- Correctional Facilities
- Family Counselors
- Inpatient Treatment Centers
- Juvenile Treatment Providers
- Marriage Counselors
- Offender Treatment Providers
- Pastors/Churches
- Probation Departments
- Psychologists
- Psychotherapists
- Shelters

- Social Service Agencies
- State Corrections Departments
- Victim Treatment Providers
- Victims Advocates (private and public)

These people and institutions will be helped by this book because it is practical, easy and effective. *Stop – Breathe – Focus* is a quick study for the learner and simple to teach. There are unlimited uses for the technique with many different types of behavior and situations.

Best of all "it works!"

The psychological condition of fear is divorced from any concrete and true immediate danger. It comes in many forms: unease, worry, anxiety, nervousness, tension, dread, phobia, and so on. This kind of psychological fear is always of something that might happen, not of something that is happening now.

–ECKHART TOLLE, *The Power of Now*

Stop – Breathe – Focus

Choose positive behavior and create the life you want! Learn and use *Stop – Breathe – Focus* and you will eliminate unwanted behaviors; manage your emotions, create options and opportunities, discover your thought patterns, build self-esteem, and reclaim your power through personal responsibility.

Stop – Breathe – Focus (*SBF*) is simple and comprehensive. Saying STOP interrupts the behavior. Specific breath work redirects your attention. Focusing allows you to turn inward for dramatic change.

You may be feeling hopeless, desperate and exhausted. You've already tried to stop the behavior that has been hurting you or others. And you have every intention to quit. Yet, it seems that you can't. What do you need to change? Here are some of the compulsive behaviors that are helped by this technique:

Impulsive/Compulsive Behaviors

- Violence against others
- Violence against self/self-mutilation
- Child Abuse
- Repetitive checking behaviors; checking lights, locks, switches, etc.

- Recurring/persistent troubling thoughts
- Excessive washing and cleaning
- Intrusive doubts
- Need for things to be in particular order
- Out of control spending
- Credit card debt
- Extremely controlling behavior toward family, friends, co-workers, others

Addictive Behaviors

- Alcohol abuse
- Drug use
- Sex Addiction
- Pornography
- Excessive Masturbation
- Gambling
- Work
- Cyber Addiction (computers)
- Bingeing and Purging
- Overeating and Starvation
- TV Watching
- Video Games
- Excessive Cosmetic Surgery
- Extreme Tattooing
- Sports
- Adrenaline Junky
- Risk Taking
- Shoplifting

Anxiety Driven Behaviors

- Post Traumatic Stress Disorder
- Panic Attacks
- Excessive Worry
- Phobias
  - ◊ Fear of Public Speaking
  - ◊ Fear of Flying
  - ◊ Fear of Traveling
  - ◊ Fear of Closed-in Places
  - ◊ Fear of Insects/Snakes/Animals
  - ◊ Fear of Heights
  - ◊ Fear of Storms/Lightening/Thunder/Floods
  - ◊ Fear of Shots/Needles
- Face Picking
- Hair Pulling
- Nail Biting
- Eye Blinking
- Lip licking
- Obsessing

Nothing in life is to be feared, it is only to be understood. Now is the time to understand more, so that we may fear less.

–MARIE CURIE

These "acting out" behaviors hurt you and those you love. You can stop them immediately by learning the *SBF* technique.

Art, Sue, Pat, Glenda, Sylvia and Jack are each caught in the swirl of one or more compulsive behaviors. Their lives are severely limited and challenged by these behaviors. Their stories will guide you through each step of the *SBF* technique.

Art just moved back home. The court issued a no contact restraining order after he pushed his wife, Sarah, down the stairs and broke her ankle. Sarah asked the court to drop the restraining order because she wants to keep the family together but she also wants Art to get help. Art says he didn't mean to hurt her but she wouldn't stop nagging him. He has trouble admitting that this wasn't the first time he was violent toward Sarah.

Sue is a young mother of three children. After 28 days in rehab and three additional months of sobriety, Sue relapsed. She has a serious neurological illness from alcoholism and her husband is afraid she will die and leave him alone with their children. Sue works with her sponsor daily and has received her 30 day chip from her Alcoholics Anonymous meetings. Sue is struggling to stay sober.

Pat has acquired $69,000 in credit card debt. He likes to wear designer jeans, enjoys fine dining, makes regular trips to Las Vegas and orders merchandise from television shopping networks. Recently he discovered online poker. The atmosphere isn't as fun and exciting as the casinos but he still gets a rush from winning. He loves how he feels when spending money and gambling. The bank is getting ready to foreclose on his house.

Glenda has several boxes of laxatives in her freezer. She was morbidly obese but has lost three hundred pounds over the last two years. Occasionally Glenda binges and follows up with laxatives and excessive exercise. Her compulsion to vomit has mostly subsided but occasionally she will revert to this old behavior and throw up after she eats. Glenda only feels good about herself when she feels really empty.

Sylvia has trouble leaving her house. It started out with panic attacks whenever she would cross a bridge. Her heart pounded and her hands trembled; she felt light-headed as if she would die. A sense of impending doom overwhelmed her and she could not drive across the bridge. The problem next extended to the grocery store. The same set of symptoms would cause her to abandon her grocery cart and leave the store. It's becoming difficult for her to go shopping anywhere and lately it's even been terrifying for her to go to work. As a single woman, she has no one else to rely on and needs her job to keep her apartment and her life afloat.

Jack is a sex addict. He started masturbating when he was a kid. Online pornography makes it easy for him to collect material to use for masturbation in the privacy of his home. He spends thousands of dollars for cyber sex. No longer aroused by his wife because she's so "ordinary," Jack cruises the night scene downtown looking for more interesting women. Twice he's had to go to the doctor to be treated for venereal disease. Recently he was arrested for soliciting a prostitute. He's in jeopardy of losing his family and his job.

What is the behavior YOU want to stop, now? You may have several behaviors that are creating problems so it is important to figure out which one is most harmful and causing dire consequences in your life.

EXERCISE: BEHAVIORS I WANT TO CHANGE

Make a list of the behaviors you need to change now. List the top five. Even if there is only one behavior that is causing problems in your life, list four that are closely related or that seem to happen when you use the first one. Example –Tim listed: getting drunk; using weed; having anonymous sex; getting into fights; experiencing hangovers

1. _____

2. _____

3. _____

4. _____

5. _____

Now ask yourself:

• Is the first one really where I need to start? Or are others on the list more important? _____

_____

• Which creates the most unpleasant consequences? _____

_____

• Are some of the behaviors dependent on other behaviors? For instance, Eddie got violent only when he'd been drinking.

• Are you committed to ending the behavior?

Yes _____ No _____

If yes, continue. If no, continue anyway. It may prepare you to be ready.

Stop!

Behavior...is almost always controllable. Except for a few things like tics and stuttering and impotence, 99.9 percent of behavior is controllable. And so you are...responsible for every single thing you do.

–David K. Reynolds

The first part of the technique is the word "Stop!" When you realize that you're in trouble and about to act out, say, "Stop" to yourself. Saying "Stop!" interrupts the pattern of behavior that hurts you. You may say it out loud or silently. It is important to say stop as well as to think it. Say it in any form helpful to you, such as: Stop! Stop It! Stop right now! Quit it! Cut it out! Or just No! Whatever works for you!

You may want to put your hand over your heart as you say "Stop!" Putting your hand to your heart brings your attention back to you rather than giving it to anyone else. Or you may put your hand up in the air as you say "Stop!" And while you put your hand to your heart or up in the air, imagine a time when you felt joyful and strong. Visualizing a particular time when you were happy and strong anchors you to a more positive and powerful state. Carry that feeling to your heart. It strengthens you.

Art is pissed. All he wants is to come home after work, have a beer and be left alone for a while. First Sarah makes him take out the garbage. Then the kids bug him. Now Sarah is asking him to help the kids with their homework while she gets supper ready. He's trying to watch the news and is close to losing it. All of a sudden he realizes what's happening and says "Shit!" Then he closes his eyes for a minute, brings his hand to his heart, and says "Stop" very quietly to himself.

Sue has just dropped her kids off at school and daycare. This is the first day in a long time she hasn't had a sick child or other commitments throughout the day. Except for a few errands, she has the day to herself. Her cousin, Mary, lives nearby and she thinks about how much fun it would be to stop by to see her. Unfortunately, Mary is one of Sue's drinking partners. Sue's husband Jerry hates Mary and the way Sue acts around her. Remembering her sobriety, Sue says "Stop" out loud and holds onto the steering wheel tightly with both hands.

Pat is online checking his email. He opens one from Vegastrips.com. They're running a special junket to his favorite Las Vegas hotel and casino: air fare, hotel room, food coupons and $200 worth of gambling dollars, all for only $500 per person. He can almost see, smell and taste the atmosphere of the place. He is ready and double-clicks on the ad. Then he pauses and says, "I need to think about this." He leans back in his chair, puts his hand over his belly and thinks "wait."

Glenda is alone and it's Saturday night. She looks through her cupboard and there isn't anything "sweet" to eat (not even brown sugar, her last resort), just some yogurt, sandwich makings and fruit. This was a busy day and she hasn't eaten since her late breakfast. Glenda's on the prowl. She decides to go to the supermarket down the street. Grabbing her jacket she heads to the elevator. As her finger reaches out to the down button, she says "No, I'm not going to do this." She puts her hand in the air with her palm out and says, "Stop, right now."

Sylvia is in the grocery store. She made it to work this morning and is on her way home. It's been a stressful day and she needs food for dinner. Actually, her pantry is empty because she hasn't been to the store in a couple of weeks. As she reaches for a gallon of milk, things seem to close in on her. She feels that horrible sense of fear descending on her. "Oh, no!" she says, "Not now!" A panic attack is beginning its devastating path through her body and mind. Sylvia says "Stop" silently to herself. She can't put her hand to her chest or hold it out at all because she's afraid to let go of the cart. It's the only thing keeping her from collapsing into a heap. "Stop" she says again, this time a little bit stronger. She repeats it again and again…

Jack is cruising, looking for action. It's Friday night and he and his wife had plans to go out. He was supposed to head home immediately after work but from the minute he put his key in the ignition he was headed downtown. He knows his wife will be furious and worried but he's caught up in his fantasy. Jack stops at a red light. Looking at the red light he says, "God, what am I doing?" He pulls over to the curb and stops. Shaking, he puts his left hand on his right wrist and rubs his forearm. He feels compelled to continue cruising but then says "Whoa, what am I doing?" and then "Stop!"

You may be thinking that if you were able to say "Stop" you wouldn't need to be working in this book. The key is to practice the technique enough that it becomes default behavior and you achieve a full understanding of yourself.

Think of a time when you were going to act out and you didn't; a time when you were able to control yourself. Remembering times like that will help you remember to say "Stop."

Situations where I was able to say "stop" to control myself:
List five times you were able to control yourself. What is the behavior you controlled and what did you do to stop yourself? Example: Pat said "wait" as he leaned back in his chair and took his hands away from the computer keyboard.

1. Behavior: _____

   Stop Action: _____

2. Behavior: _____

   Stop Action: _____

3. Behavior: _____

   Stop Action: _____

4. Behavior: _____

   Stop Action: _____

5. Behavior: _____

   Stop Action: _____

How do you feel about those times you were able to interrupt the pattern? _____

_____

_____

_____

_____

_____

Anchoring is a tool you use to associate a specific feeling with a certain part of your body. As you practice placing your hand on a particular part of your body while bringing up a certain feeling, you create an anchor. Practice putting your hand over your heart or some other place that feels right to you, and say "stop." As you put your hand over your heart, close your eyes and imagine a time when you were very happy, positive and strong: A time when your heart sang and every part of you was happy to be alive. Practice doing this several times a day for 21 days. The more you practice, the easier it is to elicit those feelings each time you put your hand over your heart.

1. Sit in a private place.

2. Place your hand over your heart or on some other part of your body that feels comfortable and easy.

3. As you place your hand over your heart, say "stop."

4. Now remember a time when you had an extremely positive attitude, one of strength, joy, power and/or freedom.

5. Notice where you place your hand _____

_____.

Remember that you can just visualize the placement of your hand when you're in a situation that would be embarrassing to let others see you do this.

• Practice placing your hands and visualizing at least five times a day at different places: home, work, driving in a car (don't close your eyes while driving), exercising, etc.

• Utilize the breathing technique while simultaneously placing your hand over your heart and you will amplify the benefits. Wow!

AWARENESS

How many times a day do you find yourself behaving unconsciously? Pretty much all day every day you act without thinking. It would be too exhausting if you had to consciously think about all the things you do during the day; brushing your teeth, taking a shower, getting dressed, eating breakfast, driving, preparing meals, and other routine tasks. And you often multi-task, doing many things at once. If you had to concentrate on everything you did, it would drive you crazy. And yet, addictive and compulsive behaviors are also automatic, trance inducing and have a ritualistic component. You need to bring these actions back to conscious awareness. Always be on the lookout for automatic behavior. Going into a trance state is one of your enemies. Your sub-conscious holds your conscious self hostage and you can do some crazy things. Some of the signs of trance are:

- Arriving at a destination with no recollection of how you got there
- Catching yourself staring into space
- Losing track of time
- Finding yourself in a situation where you wonder, "What the heck is going on here?"
- Spacing out
- Tunnel vision
- Lost in yourself
- Selective hearing/seeing
- Lack of affect (this means you show little or no emotion)

Take a moment to recall incidents that might have occurred while you were in a trance state or when events got out of control without your intention. You may include signs that seem to take place whenever this happens to you:

1. Incident _____

Signs of trance: _____

_____

2. Incident _____

Signs of trance: _____

_____

3. Incident _____

Signs of trance: _____

_____

4. Incident _____

Signs of trance: _____

_____

5. Incident _____

Signs of trance: _____

_____

BEHAVIOR CHAIN

One of the key exercises in interrupting compulsive/addictive behavior is the step-by-step ritualistic pattern I call a "behavior chain." One behavior links to another behavior which links to another behavior and so on. The earlier in your behavior chain you say "stop," the easier it is to interrupt the pattern. There are different types of acting out behaviors: behaviors that seem automatic, ritualistic, and those that seem to explode from physical, emotional, mental or spiritual triggers. Identifying each step toward that behavior is the first goal. And then you develop a personal exit strategy, either before, during or after each step. In order to get a clear understanding of your behavior chain, it is best to work backward from the problematic behavior and identify each step – even the smallest ones.

How do you discover your behavior chains? Begin by recalling your last "acting out" episode. Write down the behavior. And working backwards, list everything you did up to "acting out."

Sara was a compulsive shoplifter. She was an affluent professional woman who would steal items from high-end stores, things she didn't need or even want. When she created her behavior chain she started her chain by writing down the following (it might help you to read this section from the bottom up):

- "I went to my car, got in and drove away."
- "I put my old top on over the blue blouse and walked out of the store.
- "I tried on several blouses and decided I liked the blue silk."
- "I walked into the dressing room."
- "I picked out a couple of blouses."
- "I walked into the blouse department."
- "I strolled through the store."
- "I went into Macy's."

- "I parked in my regular area."
- "I drove into the parking garage."
- "I got into my car."

When she first wrote out her behavior chain on this episode this is where she ended. I encouraged her to go further back.

- "I left my office."
- "I decided I had enough for today."
- "I hung up the phone."
- "I said, 'Well, if there's anything I can do to help you in the future, please keep me in mind."
- "He said, We've decided to give our account to another firm."
- "I had been waiting for this call hoping that I had landed this very important client for my firm."
- "My secretary told me that Mr. Jones was on the phone."

This was the end of her second attempt. I asked her to continue.

- "It was 2:30 in the afternoon."
- "My husband called to find out where I was. I had forgotten I was supposed to meet him for lunch. He said I cared more about the job than I do for him."
- "I gave the reports to my boss."
- "I finished the reports."
- "I decided to skip lunch and drank coffee at my desk."
- "He seemed angry."
- "I told him they were almost finished."
- "My boss asked me where the reports were that were due yesterday."
- "I worked frantically on the reports my boss had asked for."
- "I got to work at 7:00 AM to finish up some reports that were due yesterday."

- "I drove to work."
- "I left the house at 6:30 a.m."
- "I had two cups of coffee while getting dressed."
- "I made coffee, drank a glass of juice, took my vitamins, and ate a piece of toast."
- "I took a shower, washed and dried my hair."
- "I got up at 5:45 a.m."

I allowed her to end her behavior chain here. However she could have continued working backwards until she was very sure that this was the beginning of the chain. Some behavior chains span several days or even weeks.

To get what you want. STOP doing what isn't working.
—DENNIS WEAVER

It's your turn to create a behavior chain. Think about a situation that turned out very badly for you. What was your behavior and what were the steps leading up to it. Pay attention to seemingly insignificant decisions that might have gone either way. Example: "I hit my wife." "I got drunk." "I binged." You may want to write about the whole situation or just use the above example.

Behavior: _____

_____

_____

_____

_____

_____

_____

_____

_____

_____

Now write down the steps leading to that behavior. Be as thorough and specific as you can. Once you have created your behavior chain, go back and write down an exit strategy for each step. Exit strategies can be saying "stop," doing breath work, changing a thought, creating a different feeling, doing something different (even one little thing can make a difference), looking at options, whatever will stop the action. Some steps may not seem to be amenable to an exit strategy but keep working on it. You may want to let ideas roll around in your head and come back later to fill them in:

Step _____

Exit option _____

Step _____

Exit option _____

Step _____

Exit option _____

Step _____

Exit option _____

Step _____

Exit option _____

Step _____

Exit option _____

Step _____

Exit option _____

Step _____

Exit option _____

Step _____

Exit option _____

Step _____

Exit option _____

Step _____

Exit option _____

Step _____

Exit option _____

Step _____

Exit option _____

Step _____

Exit option _____

Step _____

Exit option _____

Step _____

Exit option _____

Step _____

Exit option _____

Step _____

Exit option _____

Step _____

Exit option _____

Step _____

Exit option _____

Step _____

Exit option _____

Step _____

Exit option _____

Step _____

Exit option _____

Step _____

Exit option _____

Step _____

Exit option _____

Step _____

Exit option _____

Step _____

Exit option _____

Step _____

Exit option _____

Step _____

Exit option _____

If you need extra space for additional steps, please use a note pad as it is important that you complete the entire chain of events; even if it extends into the previous day or even weeks.

If you complete a behavior chain as many times as you remember "acting out" you'll develop a solid knowledge of your behavior pattern. Feel free to copy the Behavior Chain so you can use it as many times as you need.

A basic benefit of being able to say "Stop" to yourself is that you will be able to manage and regulate your actions, thoughts and feelings.

Every great mistake has a halfway moment, a split second when it can be recalled and perhaps remedied.
                                                    –PEARL S. BUCK

Breathe

There's no single more powerful – or more simple – daily
practice to further your health and well-being than breathwork.
–ANDREW WEIL, M.D.

The second part of the *SBF* technique is essential: breathe, breathe, and breathe! How do you breathe in order to change your behavior? It's a simple process. You're probably thinking, "I've been breathing all my life and I already know how to breathe." And yet, refining the way you breathe and implementing conscious breathwork can change your behavior, your attitude, your health and your life. Breathe in through the nose and out through the mouth, focusing on the breath and the count. Breathe in to the count of four and out to the count of eight. Breathe in and count in your mind...one, two, three, four. Breathe out and count in your mind... one, two, three, four, five, six, seven, eight. Continue the breathing for a minimum of five sets of breaths; more if possible. After you say "stop" to yourself, remove your hand from your chest as you do your breathwork. You can do this anywhere, in any situation. If you're not driving or doing something else that requires concentration, you can close your eyes while you breathe. It is not necessary. It just helps narrow your focus. If other thoughts or distractions enter your mind, say "thank you" and let those thoughts or distractions go while bringing your attention back to the breath. Breathe in this way until you feel yourself coming back into balance and control. There are two advantages to this breath work. The first is relaxation and balance. Stress chemicals are blocked and balance is restored to your body. The second advantage is redirection. Conscious breathing puts space and time between you and the compulsive behavior, creating changes within you that restores you to sanity and right action.

• Sitting in front of the TV with his hand on his heart and his eyes closed, **Art's** chest feels as though it's made of concrete. It is almost impossible to lift his chest to let the air flow in. He forces himself to take one deep breath. He follows it with another breath. And then another. Finally he's able to develop the rhythm. He's breathing in to the count of four, out to the count of eight. Even though he's managed five sets of breaths, he realizes he needs a few more. After eight he's settling himself down.

• **Sue** realizes she's automatically doing the breathing. But she's not counting. Even though she's driving, she can breathe, count and still be alert to what's happening on the roadway so she starts over and uses the counting. Sue has limited lung capacity due to her alcohol-induced neurological condition so she breathes in to a count of three and out to a count of six. This works for her.

• With his hand on his belly, **Pat** says, "Okay, okay, okay. I need to breathe." He gets up from his computer chair and lies down flat on the floor. Pat has found this to be the most effective way for him to breathe. It keeps his body straight and allows him to take conscious breaths…in and out.

• **Glenda** leans into the wall next to the elevator and mutters, "I don't know if I can do this breathing. It probably won't even work." But she does it anyway. In four, out eight. Five sets. She does it!

• Gripping the supermarket cart, **Sylvia** tries to do the breathing. She realizes that because she's breathing very rapidly, she's almost hyperventilating. "Slow down," she says gently to herself. "Slow down," she says again and quietly starts to count. In: two, three, four. Out: two, three, four, five, six, seven, eight. "Oh this feels so much better!" she thinks to herself as she continues to count her breaths for five sets, measuring each set on the fingers of her right hand.

• Parked at the curb, **Jack's** breathing is rapid and hard. It's almost as if he's panting. "I have to get my breathing under control," he thinks. He breathes in: one, two, and then out: one two, three, four. It gets easier with each breath. Jack increases his breathing so he breathes in to the count of three and out to the count of six. By the time he works his way up to the standard "In-four; Out-eight" routine he's feeling more in control. Jack realizes that he's now able to turn his attention inward, to focus on himself.

Breath is the bridge which connects life to consciousness, which unites your body to your thoughts.
                                            –Thich Nhat Hanh

- Sit back

- Place your hands on your belly

- Close your eyes

- Concentrate on your breath

- You want to breathe using your diaphragm. This means you allow the filament below your lungs (your diaphragm) to drop down which allows air to enter the lungs. Your belly will move out when you breathe in and will contract when you breathe out.

- Do ten sets of breaths this way. You can count each set using your fingers.

- Each time you do this exercise, increase the number of sets you do.

- Optimum time breathing in this way is at least ten minutes, twice a day.

- The more you do this – the easier it will be for you to breathe when you show signs of "acting out."

You can tell you are breathing inadequately when it is shallow; your chest rises and falls with the breath and shoulders may move up and down. When you breathe correctly, you allow your abdomen to move outward on the in-breath and then back in on the out-breath. The diaphragm is a filament that rests underneath your lungs. As you release the diaphragm, it moves down and away from the lungs, allowing the lungs to fill with air. As you compress the diaphragm it moves back up and forces air from the lungs. When you breathe in this way, the lungs are so happy because they are used to their full capacity. Are you confused? Are you wondering if you're doing the breath work correctly? If so, use the following exercise.

EXERCISE: FLOOR BREATHING

- Find space on the floor with plenty of room to lie down comfortably.

- Lie down flat on the floor. You may use a small cushion for your head and you may raise your knees if you have back problems. Note, the trunk of your body needs to be lying flat.

- Place your hands on your abdomen.

- Now begin breathing.

- You will automatically breathe correctly in this position, with the diaphragm moving as needed and no shoulder action.

- Pay attention to how it feels to breathe in this manner.

- Breathe lying on the floor until you can do it correctly sitting or standing.

The cyclone derives its powers from a calm center. So does a person.
                                    −NORMAN VINCENT PEALE

Heart meditation is one of the most successful breathing processes. It can change your urges and your problems in just minutes.

- Begin deep breathing, focusing on the breath for about five minutes.

- Breathe as though the air is moving in and out through your heart.

- Steadily and evenly, imagine the air flowing in-around-through-and out of the body by way of the heart .

- Next, remember a very happy memory, it could be an event, a beloved person or pet, or perhaps just a time when you were very peaceful, such as living near the ocean, seeing a perfect sunrise, or a hearing singing bird.

- Notice how the memory feels in your heart. Sometimes I can actually feel my heart buzz with positive energy.

- Allow yourself to continue focusing on the positive feeling in your heart as long as possible. Any errant thoughts that pop up in your mind can be thanked and released; returning over and over to the breath work and the feeling held in your heart.

- If the memory begins to create negative feelings, release them or create a new memory in your mind that won't evoke any negativity.

- Ah! How wonderful that is! And when you're finished, notice how your perspective may have changed with regard to problems or situations that were bothering you.

When do you use breath work? Whenever you recognize that stress is beginning to build you need to use the calming breath. Other times to breathe are when you're driving, working, engaging in a sport, getting ready to perform, talking with your mate, dealing with children, entering negotiations, dealing with pain, whenever you need to maximize your health and effectiveness, or when you feel triggered to "act out." I recommend setting aside ten to fifteen minutes every morning and evening so that you can begin and end your day with breathwork. In order to do this it's wise to look back on situations that occurred and figure out when you could have started the breathwork.

1. Situation: _____

    Time to breathe: _____

2. Situation: _____

    Time to breathe: _____

3. Situation: _____

    Time to breathe: _____

4. Situation: _____

    Time to breathe: _____

5. Situation: _____

    Time to breathe: _____

Over the course of each day, give yourself a break – breathe in through the nose, out through the mouth; breathe in to the count of four – out to the count of eight. Breathe deeply into the diaphragm and then completely empty the lungs on the out breath. Let go of distracting thoughts. Let go of tension and stress. Allow yourself to revel in the feeling of calm relaxation. Get in tune with your body, heart, mind and spirit. Allow yourself to feel the life coursing through your body and be glad. All is well!

You know that our breathing is the inhaling and exhaling of air. The organ that serves for this is the lungs that lie round the heart, so that the air passing through them thereby envelops the heart. Thus breathing is a natural way to the heart. And so, having collected your mind within you, lead it into the channel of breathing through which air reaches the heart and, together with this inhaled air, force your mind to descend into the heart and to remain there."

—Nicephorus the Solitary

Focus

Your soul is oftentimes a battlefield... Would that I could be the peacemaker in your soul, that I might turn the discord and the rivalry of your elements into oneness and melody. But how shall I, unless you yourselves be also the peacemakers, nay, the lovers of all your elements?"

–KAHLIL GIBRAN

The third part of the *Stop – Breathe – Focus* technique is "Focus," a short-hand term for creating awareness and options through focusing on yourself. Focus is your key to freedom: freedom from the past, freedom from fear, freedom from the chains of shame, freedom from judgment and freedom from powerlessness. Focus is how you find your true self, your reason, your heart, your physical being and the vast wonder of your spirit. Focus is your guide to awakening from unconscious living, to uncovering your inner pool of wisdom, talent, desire, intention and purpose, and to creating options that promote a positive and happy life for yourself and for those around you. Focus is your guide to knowing and loving all aspects of yourself.

I invite you on a journey of self-discovery and transformation. You are an incredible human being. Once you become aware of the miracle of who you are, and the magic to be found in your body, heart, mind and spirit, your life will change.

It has been pointed out that the human ability to reason is what separates us from the rest of creation. And yet, most of us are creatures of habit, responding to situations, people, triggers and problems automatically, without thinking about it. We are conditioned to behave in certain ways often as a result of things that happened many years ago. We let the past dictate to us how we respond in the present. Our emotions lead us into behavior that creates problems for us and becomes repetitive over time.

Moira, a client with an eating disorder, told me about a time when she was a teenager. Moira was 14 years old and had a date for homecoming. After the football game, her date expected her to walk home by herself to change clothes and then he and his mom would pick her up to take her to the dance. She told him that if she walked home by herself she would not go to the dance. He refused to walk with her. When she got home she was in tears. Moira's mom told her to go change her clothes, get into something comfortable while mom made her an orange float. Mom knew she loved orange floats. Moira realized that when things didn't go her way she tended to eat comfort food, high in calories and fat. It wasn't something she would think about, just something she did automatically. When Moira became conscious of the driving force behind much of her problematic behavior, she was able to choose a different way.

The first rule of focus is this: Wherever you are, be there.
—UNKNOWN

Hot Button Worksheet: What are some of your hot buttons and triggers? In other words, what are some of the things that people say or do that set you off? What are some of the situations that will trigger automatic problem behaviors in you? What are some places, sounds, smells, feelings, people, music or anything else that will set you off?

At Home: Spouse, Partner, Kids, Pets, etc. _____

_____

_____

_____

_____

_____

_____

_____

_____

_____

Work: Boss, Partner, Employees, Customers, Co-workers, etc. _____

_____

_____

_____

_____

_____

_____

_____

_____

Social: Friends, Sporting events, Get-togethers, Bars, Etc. _____

_____

_____

_____

_____

_____

_____

_____

Chemicals: _____

_____

_____

_____

_____

_____

Other: _____

_____

_____

_____

_____

_____

Hot Buttons and triggers are not usually a surprise. They happen over and over again. Your job is to identify as many as possible and then create a plan for responding to them in an appropriate manner.

DETACHMENT

Detachment is the act of separating from certain aspects of who you are and what is occurring within you. Unconscious living is detaching from your body, heart, mind or spirit and being unaware of what's happening in any of those aspects. This causes you to be oblivious of your behavior, how your behavior is manifesting and the effect it has on yourself and others. Detaching may be a tool used to survive years of abuse, neglect or victimization. But sometimes survival tools become a problem in themselves, creating harmful results, even contributing to addictive/compulsive behavior.

One of the best ways to figure out your pattern of detachment is to ask those closest to you. Ask them what they notice about you at certain times. You might even stop in the middle of an incident and ask those around you what they perceive.

Max is a somewhat short, very muscular and heavy set man who attended domestic violence classes. One day he came in and started yelling at me. He didn't have the money to pay for that particular session. His face was extremely red, his fists were clenched and he was standing and talking in a very aggressive manner. I asked him to look at himself and what he was doing. He became aware of what was going on with him physically and was astounded when I pointed out to him what I was experiencing as a result of his behavior. Max told me he had no idea he was coming across that way. He was scared because he didn't have the money and needed to come to classes. I told him that he had been faithfully attending, was working very hard in group, and that we could work out a payment plan. Max told me that he would work on becoming aware of himself and his effect on others.

What are the behaviors you manifest that are signs of trouble – that is escalation, "acting out," etc. Think to yourself, "What do people tell me I do, say, or look like when I'm having problems." Example: "My wife tells me that my eyebrows furrow and I get a wild look in my eyes right before I explode." Make a list of those behaviors.

_____

_____

_____

_____

I notice these things about myself – Examples: Feel like I'm outside my body; Watching myself and can't stop the action; Acting in a certain way and don't know why; Can't remember situations, behaviors, words, thoughts, etc.

_____

_____

_____

_____

_____

These are the times I became aware of the signs I detached. _____

_____

_____

_____

_____

NUMBING AND SELF-MEDICATION

Pain, anger and guilt can drive you to "numb out" or to hang out in the realm of the unconscious, You may use substances or behaviors to numb physical pain or painful feelings and thoughts. Self-medication can become a source of comfort, relief and stability. It is understandable to be tempted to use outside sources to relieve pain, any kind of pain. The number of pain relievers available is astounding. Drug stores or grocery stores carry whole sections of pain relievers. Media messages say, "Are you hurting? Take a pill" "Do you have a headache? Take a pill." Do you have joint pain? Stomach pain? Neck pain? Foot pain? Tooth pain? Back pain? Carpal Tunnel? Arthritis? The list is endless. But the message is – take something to relieve the pain.

Perhaps you turn to over-the-counter medications or prescription drugs. Or maybe you use alcohol, illicit drugs, gambling, spending, sex, over-eating, anorexia, bulimia, work, or some other behavior to cover up your pain.

In the long run, using self-medication for pain doesn't work.

What you choose to focus your mind on is critical because you will become what you think about most of the time.
                                                            –NOEL PEEBLES

What things do you use to numb-out, check-out or self-medicate?

Substances:

Alcohol (types) _____

_____

_____

_____

Drugs:

Prescription drugs: _____

_____

_____

_____

_____

Illegal drugs: _____

_____

_____

_____

_____

Over-the-counter drugs: _____

_____

_____

_____

_____

Foods: _____

_____

_____

_____

_____

Behaviors:

Financial: _____

_____

_____

_____

_____

Work: _____

_____

_____

_____

_____

Sex: _____

_____

_____

_____

_____

Gambling: _____

_____

_____

_____

Computers: _____

_____

_____

_____

_____

Video Games: _____

_____

_____

_____

_____

Television: _____

_____

_____

_____

_____

Sudoku/Crossword Puzzles: _____

_____

_____

_____

_____

Other: _____

_____

_____

_____

_____

When and where do you use these substances, thoughts, behaviors to numb or medicate yourself?

Substances:

Alcohol (types) _____

_____

_____

_____

Drugs:

Prescription drugs: _____

_____

_____

_____

_____

_____

Illegal drugs: _____

_____

_____

_____

_____

Over-the-counter drugs: _____

_____

_____

_____

_____

Foods: _____

_____

_____

_____

_____

Behaviors:

Financial: _____

_____

_____

_____

_____

Work: _____

_____

_____

_____:_____

Sex: _____

_____

_____

_____

_____

Gambling: _____

_____

_____

_____

Computers: _____

_____

_____

_____

_____

Video Games: _____

_____

_____

_____

_____

Television: _____

_____

_____

_____

_____

Sudoku/Crossword Puzzles: _____

_____

_____

_____

_____

Other: _____

_____

_____

_____

_____

As you turn toward yourself, the techniques will teach you how to identify what you're feeling and thinking; your options and their consequences; and how to develop healthy self-talk and self-responsibility. Each letter of the word **F-O-C-U-S** stands for one aspect of the process of turning inward.

I don't need anyone to rectify my existence. The most profound relationship we will ever have is the one with ourselves.

–HORST RECHELBACHER

F is for Feelings and Thoughts

Feelings and thoughts are temporary and fluid which means that they come and go. And yet we often allow feelings and thoughts to determine our behavior without full awareness of the accuracy and reliability of them. Awareness is your first step toward self-knowledge and self-control. How do you become aware of what you're feeling or thinking? It's about turning your focus inward; paying attention to yourself, putting descriptors on your feelings and clarifying your thoughts.

How do you describe what you're feeling? It is important to avoid descriptors such as "good," "bad," "great," "terrible," "awful," or "wonderful." These words are judgmental and fall under the "black or white thinking" mode. That means if you're not "good" then you're "bad." If you're "terrible" then you can't be "wonderful." And what does feeling good or bad really mean? When you say you're feeling good, does it mean that you're healthy, happy, on top of things? When you say you're feeling bad, does that mean you're sick, your cat died, you're getting a divorce or you're sad? When you use good or bad how do other people know what it means exactly? There is a list of feelings at the end of this section you can use to be specific about how you're feeling.

So take a moment, step back and figure out what's going on with you.

PHYSICAL FEELINGS

Your body is the messenger for your emotions, thoughts and sense of connection. Pay attention to what your body tells you. There are two aspects of your body awareness: the situational aspect and the sensational aspect.

Situationally, if you're "SHOT" (Sick, Hungry, Overworked, Tired), you respond differently than if you're feeling healthy, energized, well-fed, and strong. Realizing when you're "SHOT" helps you to deal with your needs so that you make wise choices.

Sometimes my feelings are so hot that I have to take the pen and put them out on paper to keep them from setting me afire inside; then all that ink and labor are wasted because I can't print the results.

–MARK TWAIN

Look at some of the physical conditions that put you in jeopardy. Check items that are present prior to or during your "acting out" behavior.

_____ Awkward

_____ Battered

_____ Broken

_____ Exhausted

_____ Fed up

_____ Feverish

_____ Full

_____ Hungry

_____ Hung over

_____ Overworked

_____ Pushed to the limit

_____ Sick

_____ Sleep Deprived

_____ Stressed

_____ Terrorized

_____ Tired

_____ Traumatized

_____ Other _____

_____

_____

_____

_____

Sensationally, body signs may be the first warning that things aren't okay with you. It's important that you become aware of your particular body warnings. Here are some warning signs.

- A knot in the stomach
- Agitation
- Antsy
- Baring your teeth
- Black spots in front of your eyes
- Clenched teeth
- Craving for an addictive substance
- Crying
- Dry mouth
- Frown lines above your nose
- Grimace
- Grinding teeth
- Hot face
- Lowered eye lids
- Narrow focus of vision
- Pain
- Pounding pulse in the ear
- Raising your voice
- Shaking your head
- Stiff neck
- Tight muscles
- Trembling

- Whining

- Wrinkle in your forehead

Physical warning signs are different with each person and each problem behavior. Realizing your early warning signs will assist you in making better choices.

Here is how Art, Sue, Pat, Glenda, Sylvia and Jack respond to physical signs of distress:

- After stopping, breathing and settling down a bit, **Art** realizes that when he clenches his hands, grits his teeth, tightens his lips, and feels heat in his face, that he's close to losing his temper. He also realizes that sometimes it feels like he has a steel strap wrapped tightly around his chest. It's almost as though he's a metal spring, wound tight and ready to explode. Art is learning about himself and feels satisfied.

- While driving, **Sue** admits to herself that she is sleep deprived. She hasn't had a full night's sleep in about a week because her youngest child has had a bad chest cold with incessant coughing and high fevers. A couple of nights in a row she's had to bathe Cody in a tepid bath to bring down the fever. She's been running on caffeine and a sense of responsibility to her family. Therefore, Sue realizes she's feeling depleted with little or no energy, she feels very heavy, the muscles in her upper back and neck are tense, and she's experiencing a lot of pain from her neuropathy. The pain is relentless and extreme when her pant legs brush against her skin. Honest reflection and expanding self-awareness creates more space between herself and the desire for a drink.

- Still on the floor, having finished five sets of breaths, **Pat** becomes aware of his agitation. He feels the adrenaline running through his system at just the thought of the junket. He gets up from the floor and sits at his computer. He notices that his eyes create a narrow focus so that all he can see is the keyboard and the screen offering the sweet deal. His fingers tremble and he feels moisture trickling down from his armpits. His lips are dry and he licks them with his tongue. Pat feels like he's getting to know himself and his body's warning signals. This feels better than "giving in" to the compulsion.

• While walking back to her apartment, **Glenda** notices that she is way too hungry! She feels a deep churning and realizes her stomach is growling. She can almost hear her stomach making demands, saying, "Feed me, I'm hungry!" She's a little dizzy and has a headache. Her whole body begins to quiver. She hasn't been this hungry in a long time.

• **Sylvia** realizes the physical sensations of her panic attacks begin with a tightening around the eyes and a feeling that her surroundings are closing in on her. She describes it to herself as dark shades being drawn around the edge of her vision. She continues to inventory her sensations: pounding heart, shakiness, weakness in her knees, dizziness, lightheadedness, sweating, a sense of choking, alternating chills/hot flashes, and pain in her chest. Her body feels like it's going to die! Sylvia's objective inventory of sensations steadies her. She is no longer gripping the shopping cart. She feels more "in control."

• **Jack** observes that he has an erection. This episode, he recounts, started out with sweaty palms, a hollow feeling in his stomach and a weird feeling in his heart. Then he feels the blood rush to his genitals and he gets hard. He feels charged, as though he has megawatts of electricity coursing through his body. This is the energy that drives him to look for sex in any form. Jack realizes the behaviors that seem to control him actually have a set ritual. The same feelings occur in the same order, with the same results, ending in the same behavior, each time he "acts out."

What are the signs that you're in jeopardy? Place a check mark next to items on the list below that pertain to you. At the end of the list, write in those that weren't mentioned.

_____ A knot in the stomach

_____ Agitated

_____ Aroused

_____ Baring your teeth

_____ Black spots in front of your eyes

_____ Charged

_____ Chills

_____ Clenched teeth

_____ Crampy / PMS'ing

_____ Craving an addictive substance

_____ Depleted

_____ Dizzy

_____ Drained

_____ Dry mouth

_____ Fidgity

_____ Frown lines above your nose

_____ Grimace

_____ Grinding teeth

_____ Headache

_____ Heavy perspiration / sweating

_____ Hot face (turning red)

_____ Jittery

_____ Lightheaded

_____ Narrow focus of vision

_____ Pain

_____ Pounding pulse in the ear

_____ Racing heart beat

_____ Shaking your head

_____ Stiff neck

_____ Strung out

_____ Sweaty / itchy palms

_____ Tight chest

_____ Trembling

_____ Voice: loud, harsh, strident

_____ Weak kneed

_____ Whining

_____ Wrinkle in your forehead

_____ Tight muscles

_____ Other _____

_____

_____

_____

_____

_____

_____

_____

EMOTIONAL FEELINGS

Love is divine power and your heart is at the center of your being, offering love wherever you may direct it. Love is the most powerful force in the universe. It can move mountains, create something out of nothing, and revitalize even the most desperate people. All of your emotions are created in your heart center. And your heart is the most powerful organ in your body. It creates vibrations which are then transformed into emotions. The slower the vibration, the more negative the emotion and conversely, the higher vibrations create more positive emotions. So, what are emotions? They are manifestations of feeling from your heart. They range from fear, depression and despair at the bottom of the spectrum, through jealousy, hatred, and rage, on up the scale to worry and doubt and finally upward to hope, happiness and finally joy and love. There are thousands of emotions you can feel. Your mandate is to create positive emotions so that you can maximize your potential for creating the life that you want.

Emotions are uncomfortable to some people. Males, particularly, are taught not to acknowledge or recognize emotions. And yet, when you are able to accurately label your feelings, awareness of yourself and others increases, and the distance between you and the compulsive behaviors you desire to eliminate becomes greater. Mad, sad, glad and scared are the four basic feelings, and there are thousands of derivatives for each of these. Inventory your emotional feelings using descriptive words, rather than the simplistic "feeling good" or "feeling bad." After becoming aware of their physical sensations, our cast of characters turns toward their emotions as they continue the Focus part of the SBF technique:

- **Art** thinks he's angry. And yet, when he spends time figuring out what's really going on with him, he realizes he's feeling a lot of things besides anger. He's feeling overwhelmed by his job, frustrated by the demands of his wife, resentful that he can't sit down and relax, and inadequate because he can't provide better for his wife and his family.

• **Sue** is feeling down, inadequate, and hopeless. The doctor has told her that her neural illness is incurable. There may be some remission but she will never recover the nerve cells that have died. Sue is also dealing with Post Acute Withdrawal (PAW), a combination of residual effects due to long-term withdrawal. Terence Gorski, in his book, *Staying Sober*, lists six symptoms of PAW:

1. Inability to think clearly

2. Memory problems

3. Emotional over-reactions or numbness

4. Sleep disturbances

5. Physical coordination problems

6. Stress sensitivity

Sue feels frustrated with herself and misses the numbing effect of alcohol.

• Opening the Vegastrips.com email, **Pat** admits to himself that he feels excited and almost high. He "loves" the feeling of stimulation he gets when planning gambling trips and buying things online. The rush he gets from the planning and anticipation are almost as good as the actual sprees themselves.

• **Glenda** hates herself. She feels weak, defective, frustrated, inadequate, intense, ugly, fat, worthless and desperate. Glenda is overwhelmed by the extensive bundle of feelings she notices inside herself. She wishes she could eat them all away but she admits to herself that eating only intensifies the feeling of being overwhelmed.

• **Sylvia** notices her fear. She doesn't want to die and yet that's what she feels will happen. Sylvia wants to run home, where she feels safe and never venture out again. She notices that she feels exhausted and at the end of her rope. She feels embarrassed and ashamed, because surely she's the only one in the world afraid to go to the grocery store or to drive over bridges.

• **Jack** is feeling numb emotionally. At first he can't come up with any emotions because he's so focused on his physical feelings. Then Jack realizes he feels desperate, frantic, and reckless. When he's as physically aroused as he is now, his emotions are frenzied and erratic. He feels totally out of control.

You cannot make yourself feel something you do not feel,
but you can make yourself do right in spite of your feelings.

–PEARL S. BUCK

What are you feeling emotionally when you "act out?" Remember that you might manifest anger when another feeling is at the root of your behavior. Our society promotes the use of anger rather than fear, hurt, frustration, disappointment, embarrassment, shame, guilt, etc. Make a list of some of the feelings you recognize as a pattern when you've been "acting out" (see the list at the end of this section to help you identify feelings).

_____

_____

_____

_____

_____

_____

_____

_____

_____

_____

_____

Which of your feelings create the most problems for you? _____

_____

_____

_____

_____

_____

MENTAL FEELINGS

There is nothing more fertile than your mind. It is always creating. That which is in your mind becomes your reality. What power! What genius! You might be thinking, "I'm certainly no genius!" And yet you have the capacity to create whatever reality you want. There is a universal law at work in your mind. It is the Law of Attraction. The Law of Attraction basically states that you attract whatever you have created within you. Like attracts like. It is a very simple concept and yet many people are not aware of it or they think it's a lot of hooey. You may notice that when your thoughts are positive, when they are creative, your life runs a little smoother, good things happen to you, it's a little easier to reach the goals you've set for yourself. Conversely, when you're down in the dumps, everything seems to go wrong.

What's going on in your mind? Believe it or not, your mind can feel. Feeling negative, obsessive, destructive, positive, creative, and healthy are examples of mental feelings. The Focus step of the SBF technique helps you to realize when you're focusing on the negative aspects of a situation, and to become aware when you're thinking the same destructive thoughts over and over again...thoughts that lead to the compulsive behaviors you desperately want to eliminate from your life and you can't let go. Conscious awareness to the tone of your thoughts allows you to change from negativity to a positive and proactive mindset.

• **Art** becomes aware that mentally he is spiraling downward. He looks at himself and everyone else with a negative filter. This effects his emotions, causing pessimism and disapproval to be a continual state of mind.

• **Sue** recognizes her mental state as foggy and scattered. Post Acute Withdrawal affects her ability to have clear concise thoughts and keeps her somewhat confused and muddled.

She finds herself jumping from one thing to another and losing track of time. She doesn't remember a time when she wasn't feeling befuddled.

• Mentally, **Pat** associates his feelings with looking through the wrong end of a telescope. He has a clear focus only on his trip. Everything else is peripheral or out of reach.

• **Glenda** shifts attention to her mental feelings and finds that desperation and fixation are the primary tone.

• **Sylvia** is able to name her mental feelings; hopelessness, helplessness and inability to concentrate on anything other than her fear. It dominates her mind completely.

• **Jack** finds that he is totally obsessed and uncontrollable mentally. "So this is what is meant by thinking only with your penis," he says when he figures out his mental state.

The feeling of being valuable – 'I am a valuable person' – is essential to mental health and is a cornerstone of self-discipline.
–M. SCOTT PECK

What is your mental state prior to, during and post "acting out?" Looking back on your behavior what was the mental attitude from which you were operating?

Example: Negativity, obsession, depression, mania, grandiosity, judgmental, critical, unrealistic expectations. Look back over many episodes to see if there is a correlation.

Situation 1:

Episode: _____

_____

_____

_____

_____

_____

Mental State: _____

_____

_____

Situation 2:

Episode: _____

_____

_____

_____

_____

_____

Mental State: _____

_____

_____

Situation 3:

Episode: _____

_____

_____

_____

_____

_____

_____

Mental State: _____

_____

_____

Situation 4:

Episode: _____

_____

_____

_____

_____

_____

Mental State: _____

_____

_____

Episode: _____

_____

_____

_____

_____

_____

_____

Mental State: _____

_____

_____

SPIRITUAL FEELINGS

Your spiritual aspect is the life source energy that courses through your body, heart and mind. It is the intelligent connection that flows through every living thing and every inert object. There is nothing in the universe that doesn't have that divine intelligence manifesting within. We are all one. Some people believe that, others don't. And yet there is a connection that is hard to explain. I have a couple of toy Care Bears that have magnets in their paws. When the magnets are connected and the bears seem to be holding hands, they sing a song together. When one of the paws is disconnected, the singing stops. I ask my clients to hold hands in my groups. Then I put the two Care Bears between different people. When all hands are connected, the bears sing, if one person lets go of another person's hand, the singing stops. It doesn't matter where in the circle this occurs. The magnetic current travels through all of us and if a disconnection occurs, the singing stops immediately.

Spiritually using the SBF technique refers to connection, not religion nor God. People connect or disconnect in many ways. You may feel connected with your Higher Power or God. You may feel connected with pets and other animals. Or you may seek connection with nature, other people or even with yourself. Much compulsive behavior is associated with a feeling of alienation, isolation, loneliness, or disconnection. However, many people are not even aware that a sense of isolation pervades their being.

- Spiritually, **Art** faces feeling unlovable and unloved. "I'm such an asshole, how can anyone love me?" or "If they loved me, they would do what I want."

- **Sue** identifies a feeling of separation; feeling so very alone and disconnected from everyone and everything. No one understands her pain, both physical and emotional. No one appreciates her.

- **Pat** is beginning to understand that the excitement and exhilaration he feels from spending and gambling is the only time he feels connected. And yet, he understands that it is a false sense of connection. In everyday life he's bored, lonely and disconnected.

- **Glenda** feels that she's the only person on earth that is going through such misery. She also feels a sense of alienation from "normal" people who have never had a weight problem. They don't know what she's had to go through.

- "Disconnected, that's me spiritually," thinks **Sylvia**. Since her mother passed away, Sylvia's been alone and detached from everyone. Lately people have been stepping in and helping her, going to the store for her, following her to work, and checking in on her.

• **Jack** is looking for connection in his searching for sexual fulfillment. Ironically, the more he acts out, the more isolated he feels. His estrangement from his wife doubles his isolation as she was the only person with whom he had any sense of belonging.

To make the right choices in life, you have to get in touch with your soul. To do this, you need to experience solitude, which most people are afraid of, because in the silence you hear the truth and know the solutions.

-DEEPAK CHOPRA

Identify the negative "spiritual connection" feelings you experience during an "acting out" episode:

_____

_____

_____

_____

What can you do to reclaim connection? Examples: pray, call a friend or your sponsor, talk with a loving family member, use affirmations, etc. You know best when you feel a healthy sense of connection. List a few things you can do to get connected.

_____

_____

_____

_____

_____

_____

> *Happiness canot be traveled to, owned, earned, worn or consumed. Happiness is the spiritual experience of living every minute with love, grace and gratitude.*
> —DENIS WAITLEY

Create an emergency kit. When you're heading towards "acting out" and you're feeling disconnected, an emergency kit can help. Here are some things that you can put in a zip lock bag or any other container that would be handy for you:

- Picture of loved ones (kids, spouse, pets, parents, family, friends, other loved ones)
- Meaningful reading
- List of reasons to refrain from "acting out" (you created this list at an earlier time)
- Prayers
- Telephone list (sponsors, friends, helpful people, etc.)
- Band-aid (superman band-aids are cool) to heal wounds
- CD of inspirational song
- Symbol of hope (arrowhead, cross, anything to create hope in your heart)
- Affirmations list – choose affirmations that will be effective to help you reconnect
- Hershey's Kiss
- Other (anything that will create connection or hope)

FEELINGS LIST

Below is a comprehensive list of feelings. You may want to look through the list and put a check mark next to any of the feelings you experience when heading toward trouble.

____Abandoned	____Achy	____Adrift
____Absorbed	____Action oriented	____Adulterated
____Abundant	____Adamant	____Affected

_____Affectionate	_____Appalled	_____Bamboozled
_____Afflicted	_____Appealing	_____Banished
_____Afraid	_____Appreciative	_____Bastardized
_____Aggravated	_____Apprehensive	_____Battered
_____Aggressive	_____Approachable	_____Beastly
_____Agitated	_____Argumentative	_____Beaten
_____Agonizing	_____Arrogant	_____Beat Up
_____Agreeable	_____Artful	_____Beautiful
_____Alarmed	_____Ashamed	_____Becoming
_____Alienated	_____Asinine	_____Befuddled
_____Alone	_____Aspiring	_____Beholden
_____Ambiguous	_____Assaulted	_____Belittled
_____Ambitious	_____Assertive	_____Belligerent
_____Amiable	_____Assured	_____Belonging
_____Amused	_____Astonished	_____Beloved
_____Angry	_____Astounded	_____Bemused
_____Animated	_____Attentive	_____Beneficent
_____Animosity	_____Attitudinal	_____Benevolent
_____Annihilated	_____Attractive	_____Berated
_____Annoyed	_____Avid	_____Berserk
_____Anonymous	_____Awake	_____Besieged
_____Antagonized	_____Awesome	_____Betrayed
_____Antsy	_____Awful	_____Bewildered
_____Anxious	_____Awkward	_____Bewitched
_____Apathetic	_____Badly	_____Biased
_____Apologetic	_____Baffled	_____Bilious

_____Bitchy

_____Biting

_____Bitten

_____Bitter

_____Bizarre

_____Blackmailed

_____Blameless

_____Blameworthy

_____Blank

_____Blasphemous

_____Bleak

_____Blessed

_____Blinded

_____Blissful

_____Bloated

_____Blocked

_____Bloodied

_____Blown Away

_____Blown Off

_____Blown Over

_____Blue

_____Blunt

_____Boastful

_____Blurry

_____Bogged Down

_____Boggled

_____Boiling

_____Boisterous

_____Bold

_____Bonkers

_____Boorish

_____Boring

_____Bottomed Out

_____Bound Up

_____Brainless

_____Brainwashed

_____Brash

_____Brave

_____Brazen

_____Breathless

_____Brilliant

_____Brisk

_____Broken

_____Brokenhearted

_____Brought Down

_____Bruised

_____Brushed Off

_____Brutalized

_____Brutish

_____Bubbly

_____Bullied

_____Buoyant

_____Burdened

_____Burned Out

_____Bushed

_____Butchered

_____Buttery

_____Bypassed

_____Callous

_____Calm

_____Capable

_____Capricious

_____Cared About

_____Cared For

_____Careful

_____Careless

_____Catalyzed

_____Cautious

_____Celibate

_____Cerebral

_____Certain

_____Challenged

_____Charitable

_____Charming

_____Chaste

_____Cheap

_____Cheated

_____Cheerful

_____Childish _____Competitive _____Contrary

_____Childlike _____Complacent _____Contrite

_____Chilled _____Compliant _____Controversial

_____Chilly _____Composed _____Convicted

_____Chirpy _____Compressed _____Convinced

_____Chivalrous _____Compromised _____Cool

_____Choked Up _____Compulsive _____Cooperative

_____Civil _____Conceited _____Corrupted

_____Classy _____Concerned _____Courageous

_____Clear _____Condemned _____Courteous

_____Clever _____Confident _____Covetous

_____Close _____Conflicted _____Cowardly

_____Clumsy _____Confounded _____Crabby

_____Coarse _____Confrontational _____Cramped

_____Cocky _____Confused _____Crampy

_____Coddled _____Congenial _____Crass

_____Coerced _____Connected _____Crazy

_____Cognizant _____Considerate _____Creative

_____Cold _____Conspicuous _____Credible

_____Combative _____Constrained _____Creepy

_____Comfortable _____Constricted _____Crimped

_____Commendable _____Constructive _____Crippled

_____Committed _____Contaminated _____Critical

_____Compatible _____Contented _____Criticized

_____Compelled _____Contemptuous _____Cross

_____Competent _____Contemptible _____Crossed

_____Crowded

_____Crucified

_____Crude

_____Cruel

_____Crummy

_____Cuckoo

_____Cuddly

_____Culpable

_____Cumbersome

_____Cunning

_____Curious

_____Cursed

_____Curtailed

_____Cute

_____Cynical

_____Daffy

_____Daft

_____Damaged

_____Damned

_____Dazed

_____Dazzled

_____Deadened

_____Debauched

_____Debilitated

_____Deceived

_____Deceptive

_____Decisive

_____Decrepit

_____Dedicated

_____Defensive

_____Defiant

_____Deficient

_____Defiled

_____Definite

_____Deflated

_____Defrauded

_____Defunct

_____Defused

_____Degenerate

_____Degraded

_____Dehumanized

_____Dejected

_____Delighted

_____Delinquent

_____Delirious

_____Deluded

_____Demanding

_____Demented

_____Demolished

_____Demoralized

_____Dependent

_____Depleted

_____Depraved

_____Depreciated

_____Depressed

_____Deprived

_____Desecrated

_____Deserted

_____Deserving

_____Desirable

_____Desirous

_____Desolate

_____Despairing

_____Desperate

_____Despicable

_____Despised

_____Despondent

_____Destined

_____Detached

_____Determined

_____Devastated

_____Devilish

_____Devious

_____Devoted

_____Diabolic

_____Dictatorial

_____Diffident

_____Dignified

_____Dilapidated   _____Disobedient   _____Earnest

_____Diligent   _____Disorganized   _____Easy

_____Diminished   _____Dispassionate   _____Ebullient

_____Diplomatic   _____Dispensable   _____Ecstatic

_____Disaffected   _____Dissatisfied   _____Edgy

_____Disarmed   _____Dissuaded   _____Eerie

_____Discarded   _____Distracted   _____Effeminate

_____Disconnected   _____Distraught   _____Egotistic

_____Disconsolate   _____Distressed   _____Elated

_____Discontented   _____Distrustful   _____Electrified

_____Discouraged   _____Disturbed   _____Elegant

_____Discourteous   _____Divine   _____Elevated

_____Discredited   _____Docile   _____Eliminated

_____Discreet   _____Dominated   _____Eloquent

_____Disgraced   _____Domineering   _____Emancipated

_____Disgusted   _____Doomed   _____Empathic

_____Disheartened   _____Dopey   _____Emphatic

_____Dishonest   _____Doubtful   _____Empty

_____Dishonorable   _____Drained   _____Enamored

_____Disillusioned   _____Dreamy   _____Encouraged

_____Disinterested   _____Driven   _____Endangered

_____Disliked   _____Dubious   _____Endeared

_____Disloyal   _____Dumb   _____Energetic

_____Dismal   _____Dumbfounded   _____Energized

_____Dismayed   _____Dutiful   _____Engrossed

_____Dismissed   _____Eager   _____Engulfed

_____Enlightened	_____Fabulous	_____Festive
_____Enraged	_____Facetious	_____Fettered
_____Enslaved	_____Faint	_____Feverish
_____Entangled	_____Faithful	_____Fickle
_____Entombed	_____Faithless	_____Fidgety
_____Envious	_____Fallible	_____Fiendish
_____Erotic	_____Fallow	_____Fierce
_____Estranged	_____Famished	_____Filthy
_____Ethical	_____Fanatical	_____Firm
_____Evasive	_____Fantastic	_____Fit
_____Evil	_____Fascinated	_____Fixated
_____Exacerbated	_____Fascinating	_____Flabbergasted
_____Exceptional	_____Fashionable	_____Flaky
_____Excitable	_____Fast	_____Flamboyant
_____Exhausted	_____Fastidious	_____Flattered
_____Exhilarated	_____Fat	_____Flatulent
_____Exiled	_____Fatigued	_____Flexible
_____Exonerated	_____Faulted	_____Flighty
_____Expansive	_____Faultless	_____Flippant
_____Experienced	_____Favorable	_____Foolish
_____Exploited	_____Fearful	_____Forgotten
_____Explosive	_____Fearless	_____Forlorn
_____Exposed	_____Feeble	_____Forsaken
_____Expressionless	_____Feisty	_____Fragile
_____Expressive	_____Feminine	_____Framed
_____Exuberant	_____Ferocious	_____Frank

_____Frantic

_____Fraudulent

_____Freakish

_____Free

_____Freed

_____Freezing

_____Fretful

_____Friendly

_____Frightened

_____Frigid

_____Frolicsome

_____Frugal

_____Frustrated

_____Fucked Up

_____Full

_____Fulfilled

_____Furious

_____Futile

_____Fuzzy

_____Gallant

_____Gassy

_____Generous

_____Ghastly

_____Giggly

_____Glamorous

_____Glowing

_____Graceful

_____Gracious

_____Grateful

_____Grandiose

_____Great

_____Grumpy

_____Guarded

_____Guilty

_____Gullible

_____Haggard

_____Handicapped

_____Handsome

_____Happy

_____Harassed

_____Hardened

_____Harmful

_____Harmless

_____Hazy

_____Healthy

_____Heartbroken

_____Heartless

_____Heavy

_____Hideous

_____Homicidal

_____Honorable

_____Honored

_____Hopeless

_____Horny

_____Hot

_____Humane

_____Humiliated

_____Humorous

_____Hung Over

_____Hungry

_____Hunted

_____Hurt

_____Hurting

_____Hysterical

_____Imaginative

_____Immoral

_____Immovable

_____Immune

_____Impetuous

_____Impious

_____Implicated

_____Important

_____Inclusive

_____Indebted

_____Indecisive

_____Indentured

_____Indignant

_____Inexcusable

_____Infatuated	_____Less than	_____Militant
_____Inferior	_____Lethal	_____Mindless
_____Infuriated	_____Lethargic	_____Mischievous
_____Injured	_____Liberated	_____Miserable
_____Inquisitive	_____Limp	_____Misguided
_____Inspired	_____Listless	_____Morbid
_____Insulted	_____Logical	_____Moronic
_____Intelligent	_____Lonely	_____Motivated
_____Intimidated	_____Longing	_____Mystified
_____Introverted	_____Loose	_____Naïve
_____Invisible	_____Lost	_____Naughty
_____Invulnerable	_____Lousy	_____Nauseous
_____Irresponsible	_____Loved	_____Needed
_____Irritable	_____Lucky	_____Nervous
_____Irritated	_____Lustful	_____Nostalgic
_____Itchy	_____Lyrical	_____Numb
_____Jealous	_____Magnetic	_____Obliterated
_____Jittery	_____Magnificent	_____Obscure
_____Jovial	_____Majestic	_____Obsessed
_____Jubilant	_____Malformed	_____Offended
_____Jumpy	_____Malicious	_____Old
_____Justified	_____Marked	_____Oppressed
_____Knotted Up	_____Marvelous	_____Optimistic
_____Lackadaisical	_____Melancholy	_____Ostracized
_____Lavish	_____Mellow	_____Outstanding
_____Lecherous	_____Miffed	_____Outwitted

_____Overcome   _____Patient   _____Playful

_____Overconfident   _____Patriotic   _____Pleasant

_____Overcritical   _____Patronizing   _____Pleasing

_____Overcrowded   _____Peaceful   _____Pliable

_____Overexcited   _____Peculiar   _____Plucky

_____Overextended   _____Pedantic   _____PMS'y

_____Overindulgent   _____Penetrating   _____Poetic

_____Overjoyed   _____Penitent   _____Polluted

_____Overlooked   _____Perceptive   _____Pompous

_____Overrated   _____Perfect   _____Poor

_____Overrun   _____Perky   _____Popular

_____Overshadowed   _____Permissive   _____Possessed

_____Overwhelmed   _____Persecuted   _____Potent

_____Painful   _____Personable   _____Powerful

_____Pampered   _____Persuaded   _____Powerless

_____Panic-stricken   _____Persuasive   _____Pragmatic

_____Paralyzed   _____Perturbed   _____Prankish

_____Pardonable   _____Perverse   _____Precarious

_____Parochial   _____Perverted   _____Prejudiced

_____Parsimonious   _____Pessimistic   _____Preoccupied

_____Partial   _____Petrified   _____Prepared

_____Passé   _____Petty   _____Preposterous

_____Passionate   _____Philanthropic   _____Prominent

_____Passive   _____Pigheaded   _____Prosperous

_____Paternal   _____Pious   _____Proud

_____Pathetic   _____Pitiless   _____Provoked

_____Pulled

_____Pure

_____Put Out

_____Puzzled

_____Quarrelsome

_____Queasy

_____Quiet

_____Radiant

_____Radical

_____Ready

_____Reassured

_____Rebellious

_____Reflective

_____Reformed

_____Relaxed

_____Reliable

_____Relieved

_____Religious

_____Reluctant

_____Remorseful

_____Remorseless

_____Reprehensible

_____Resentment

_____Resigned

_____Resilient

_____Resolute

_____Resourceful

_____Respectable

_____Responsible

_____Restless

_____Restrained

_____Retarded

_____Reticent

_____Revengeful

_____Reverent

_____Ridiculous

_____Romantic

_____Rotten

_____Rowdy

_____Ruthless

_____Sacred

_____Sacrilegious

_____Sad

_____Sadistic

_____Safe

_____Sanctimonious

_____Sarcastic

_____Satisfied

_____Scandalized

_____Scared

_____Secretive

_____Secure

_____Sedate

_____Self-confident

_____Selfish

_____Self-made

_____Self-reliant

_____Self-sufficient

_____Senile

_____Sensational

_____Sensible

_____Sentimental

_____Separate

_____Separated

_____Serious

_____Sexy

_____Sexualized

_____Shaky

_____Shallow

_____Shameful

_____Shameless

_____Shattered

_____Shocked

_____Shrewd

_____Shy

_____Sick

_____Sincere

_____Sinful

_____Skeptical	_____Stiff	_____Swollen
_____Slack	_____Stimulated	_____Sympathetic
_____Sleazy	_____Stinky	_____Tainted
_____Sleepy	_____Stodgy	_____Tempted
_____Slippery	_____Stoned	_____Tender
_____Slothful	_____Stony	_____Tense
_____Sluggish	_____Strained	_____Tentative
_____Smart	_____Stranded	_____Terrible
_____Smooth	_____Stretched	_____Terrific
_____Smothered	_____Strung Out	_____Terrified
_____Sociable	_____Stubborn	_____Terrorized
_____Sore	_____Studious	_____Thankful
_____Sorry	_____Stuffed	_____Thoughtless
_____Special	_____Stumped	_____Threatened
_____Speechless	_____Stupendous	_____Thrilled
_____Spent	_____Stupid	_____Tickled
_____Spiritual	_____Suave	_____Tight
_____Spiteful	_____Sublime	_____Tired
_____Splendid	_____Subversive	_____Tormented
_____Spooky	_____Suffocated	_____Tortured
_____Spunky	_____Suicidal	_____Touched
_____Squashed	_____Superstitious	_____Tranquil
_____Squeamish	_____Surprised	_____Transformed
_____Squeezed	_____Suspicious	_____Trapped
_____Static	_____Swan-like	_____Tricked
_____Sticky	_____Swindled	_____Triumphant

_____Troubled

_____Ugly

_____Unbalanced

_____Unbearable

_____Unbiased

_____Unburdened

_____Uncertain

_____Uncomfortable

_____Understood

_____Undesirable

_____Uneasy

_____Unemotional

_____Unethical

_____Unfaithful

_____Unforgiving

_____Unfortunate

_____Unfriendly

_____Unglued

_____Ungrateful

_____Unheard

_____Unimportant

_____Uninspired

_____Uninterested

_____Unlucky

_____Unmotivated

_____Unpopular

_____Unprepared

_____Unpretentious

_____Unproductive

_____Unprofessional

_____Unsettled

_____Unstable

_____Unwanted

_____Unwilling

_____Upset

_____Used

_____Vague

_____Valiant

_____Vanquished

_____Vengeful

_____Vexed

_____Vibrant

_____Vicious

_____Victimized

_____Vindictive

_____Violent

_____Virtuous

_____Volatile

_____Vulnerable

_____Whacked Out

_____Warm

_____Washed Out

_____Wasted

_____Weak

_____Whimsical

_____Whipped

_____Wiggly

_____Wonderful

_____Wretched

_____Zany

_____Zip

THOUGHTS

Thoughts are the chalkboard of your belief system. What you think is what you are. Aligning your thoughts and feelings with what you need and desire is a powerful form of creation. Henry Ford said, "If you think you can do something or think you can't, you're right." Pay attention to your self-talk! Deliberately choose what you think! Focus on what you want, how you might already have what you want, and create loving gratitude in your heart that anything is possible.

Remember, what you give your attention to becomes prominent in your life. If you have goals and desires, focus on the positive aspects of those goals and desires. Focusing your attention on the lack of what you want will increase that lack. For instance, if you're an alcoholic frustrated by not having wine with dinner, and you focus on the lack of wine, you will shortly be drinking wine. However, if you realize that you can drive home with no worries of being stopped, that you'll wake up in the morning with great energy, that your restaurant bill will be half of what it is when you have wine with dinner and that you'll feel powerful and free by abstaining, then chances are you're more likely to refrain from drinking.

Your thoughts are the creative force of the universe. When they are in alignment with your true self, you feel positive. When they are out of alignment with your true self, you feel negative. If you're feeling depressed, angry, frustrated, disappointed, critical of self or others, check out the thoughts that are causing these feelings. You may say that you're feeling those feelings because certain situations or people are causing you to feel that way. However, if you take a hard look at your thinking patterns, your thoughts, and your self-talk, you will discover that they are determining how you feel.

This is an incredibly powerful truth. If you want to change your life, change your thinking! When you understand the power you have to create, using your thoughts, you realize nothing is impossible; the world is full of possibilities and opportunities; for every ending there is a new beginning; and you are, indeed, the creator of your life and your reality.

What is your self- talk like? Which thoughts do you use when you're "acting out?? How are these thoughts related to your behavior? Our six friends discover the "Stinking-thinking" that creates problems for them:

- **Art's** thinking is pretty much the same as usual. Putting himself in the victim mode, he says in his mind

  ◊ "Jeez, I'm busting my butt at work all day. "

  ◊ "All I want is to come home, eat my supper and have a little peace."

  ◊ "Is that too much to ask?"

  ◊ "Instead I get home and she's on my back all the time."

  ◊ "Take out the garbage."

  ◊ "Help the kids."

  ◊ "I don't even get a chance to relax!"

  ◊ "I'm the man of the house."

  ◊ "I should be able to do what I want without being nagged all the time."

- Tired of feeling like she's in a fog, the following thoughts bring **Sue** to the brink of relapse:

  ◊ "I've been sober for over a month now and my life isn't any better."

  ◊ "My kids have been sick and it's wearing me out."

  ◊ "I'm not getting any more sleep than when I was drinking and I'm not having any fun."

◊ "I'm too young to be tied down like this."

◊ "I have cousins and friends who go out for a few drinks and some recreation, why can't I?"

◊ "Here I am running errands, taking care of kids and never have a day to myself."

◊ "God, this neuropathy is so painful, I can hardly stand it."

◊ "When will it end?"

◊ "I'm no good to anybody, especially me!"

◊ "There must be something wrong with me that my life is so bad!"

• **Pat** creates problems for himself with the following self-talk:

◊ "I really need to get away from all this."

◊ "All I face everyday is figuring out how I'm going to pay my bills and worrying about when they're going to evict me from my own house."

◊ "My job is boring and I don't make much money."

◊ "If I could make a killing in Vegas I would be able to keep my house and pay off my credit cards."

◊ "Maybe I'll become a professional gambler. I mean, that's what I'm good at and it would be great to feel up all the time."

• **Glenda's** mantra goes something like this:

◊ "I am soooo hungry! I could eat an elephant!"

◊ "No, I am an elephant. I'm so huge I shouldn't be eating anything."

◊ "It's not fair that Cathy can eat everything. She eats and drinks all the things that I love and she doesn't gain an ounce."

◊ "All I have to do is look at food and I gain weight."

◊ "It's just not fair."

◊ "What difference does it make anyway? Nobody else cares what I look like."

◊ "Maybe I'll just go to the store and get chips and ice cream. I love salty and sweet together!"

◊ "Maybe they have some carrot cake. That would be great. I love cream cheese icing and it does have carrots and nuts in it so it's not completely bad for you."

• **Sylvia** wonders if everyone is looking at her. She has a terrible feeling that people are pointing at her and noticing that she's ready to faint. Her thoughts go like this:

◊ "They must think I'm stupid, weird or strange."

◊ "Maybe they won't let me come in their store anymore if I make a scene."

◊ "They'll probably call an ambulance and I'll be taken away."

◊ "How will I get my car home? I can't afford an ambulance ride or the emergency room fees."

◊ "My knees feel like they're going to give way. I might just collapse right here on this spot."

◊ "Somebody might look up my skirt. What if it comes up around my waist? Then I'll be exposed for everyone to see."

◊ "This is terrible."

• **Jack** thinks his behavior is normal. "What guy doesn't

want sex?" he says. He remembers when he first heard about sex addiction saying, "Well, if I'm going to have an addiction, that's the one I want." Jack doesn't recall a time when he didn't think about sex. This time his mental running commentary sounds something like this:

◊ "Oh, man, I feel tense and tight. A little sex would be great."

◊ "Maybe I'll just take a quick cruise past the strip and see if there's any action going on."

◊ "I know I can't count on Nancy to take care of my needs. She's so mad at me now there's no way she'll have sex with me."

◊ "I wouldn't have to do this if my needs were met at home."

◊ "She hasn't liked sex since the day we walked down the aisle."

◊ "Besides, this won't take long. It'll be a quickie."

◊ "Oh man, I can't believe I'm such a shit!"

What is your self-talk that is a catalyst to your "acting out" behavior? You might say you aren't thinking about anything when you act out or you don't know what your thoughts/self-talk are. It is just a matter of paying attention or looking back on situations to become aware of them. Make a list of what your self-talk is.

Situation: _____

_____

_____

Self-talk: _____

_____

_____

_____

_____

_____

Situation: _____

_____

_____

Self-talk: _____

_____

_____

_____

_____

_____

Situation: _____

_____

_____

Self-talk: _____

_____

_____

_____

_____

_____

_____

Situation: _____

_____

_____

Self-talk: _____

_____

_____

_____

_____

_____

Situation: _____

_____

_____

Self-talk: _____

_____

_____

_____

_____

_____

_____

_____

Situation: _____

_____

_____

Self-talk: _____

_____

_____

_____

_____

_____

_____

Self-discipline begins with the mastery of your thoughts. If you don't control what you think, you can't control what you do. Simply, self-discipline enables you to think first and act afterward.

—NAPOLEON HILL

Man is but the product of his thoughts, what he thinks, he becomes.

—MAHATMA GANDHI

O is for Options

Options are choices. And choice is the ability to choose among alternative feelings, thoughts, perceptions, beliefs, actions, behaviors and situations.

Everyone has choices. You have choices, even in the moments when you feel stuck or trapped, when you believe there is no way out, when you see yourself as a victim, when it's like you're caught on a fast moving train over which you have no control, when you feel compelled to behave a certain way even though it is harmful to you or others, when it seems as though someone or something else is calling the shots, when things are spinning out of control, or when the future appears to be so bleak that you say to yourself, "What's the use looking for options? It won't make a difference anyway!" At these times it seems like there are no other options; or that your options are very limited. Your perception about options is skewed and you're limited to acting out in the same old way.

When faced with a craving, a burning desire to "act out," or a behavior that seems to automatically happen, you may think you have only two choices—to "act out" or to not "act out." The truth is that in every given situation there are at least three options from which to choose. Even an animal in the wild, when faced with eminent danger, has at least three options. The animal can turn away and flee; face the danger and fight; or freeze – which is essentially

– do nothing. Figuring out as many options as you can gives you several alternatives to problem behavior. You may want to sit down and write out all the options you can think of. The more options you come up with – the healthier the alternatives. You can try brainstorming options with another person.

- **Art** - Some Options
    1. Take out the trash and help the kids with their homework.
    2. Sit and read the paper while ignoring his wife and kids.
    3. Throw the trash at his wife and rub her face in it.
    4. Leave the house angry and go get drunk.
    5. Talk with his wife and tell her he'll take out the trash and help the kids with their homework but first he needs to chill out for about half an hour.

- **Sue** - Some Options
    1. Go to Mary's and say "Let's party!"
    2. Stop at a liquor store and buy a bottle of vodka.
    3. Continue on with her errands.
    4. Go to an AA Meeting.
    5. Call her sponsor.
    6. Go home, take a nice warm bath, follow that with some soft music, reading and a restful nap.

- **Pat** - Some Options
    1. Book his Vegas trip.
    2. Call his credit counselor.
    3. Spend time working on his debt plan.

4. Go to the gym and work on the free weights.

5. Go online to see if there's anything else on which he would rather spend his money.

- **Glenda** - Some Options

  1. Buy binge food and eat it.

  2. Use the food she has in her apartment to make herself a healthy dinner.

  3. Go to bed and forget about everything.

  4. Eat something healthy and then sit down and write out a food plan that prevents her from getting too hungry.

  5. Call her sponsor in her Eating Disorders Anonymous group.

- **Sylvia** - Some Options

  1. Allow herself to collapse in a heap in the middle of the grocery store, giving in to her panic attack.

  2. Run out to her car and drive home.

  3. Use the tools that she has learned and trust that the panic attack is simply her body running amok.

  4. Continue shopping in spite of her dreadful fear.

  5. Find a place to sit down and pull herself together.

- Jack - Some Options

  1. Continue cruising until he finds a score.

  2. Go home and follow through on his commitments to his wife.

  3. Call his sponsor in Sex Addicts Anonymous.

  4. Pull out his emergency kit that he uses to fight his urges.

  5. Stop at a bar and have a drink.

A critical factor when exploring your options is being clear about what you want, what your values are and what is in your best interest in the long run. These factors may seem insignificant when you're in the throes of "acting out" and yet, they're of ultimate importance.

What do you want? Make a list of what you want in life. Think large!

Relationship _____

_____

_____

_____

_____

Family _____

_____

_____

_____

_____

Work _____

_____

_____

_____

Finances _____

_____

_____

_____

Health _____

_____

_____

_____

Exercise _____

_____

_____

_____

_____

Your body _____

_____

_____

_____

_____

Recreation _____

_____

_____

_____

_____

Time off _____

_____

_____

_____

_____

Other _____

_____

_____

_____

_____

What is important to you?

_____	Achievement	_____	Importance
_____	Alone time	_____	Justice
_____	Automobiles	_____	Laughter
_____	Dependable transportation	_____	Love
		_____	Money
_____	Beautiful home	_____	Order
_____	Belonging	_____	Peace
_____	Career	_____	Power
_____	Children	_____	Recreation
_____	Comfort	_____	Religion
_____	Entertainment	_____	Responsibility
_____	Excitement	_____	Safety
_____	Fairness	_____	Sleep
_____	Family	_____	Spirituality
_____	Food	_____	Success
_____	Friends	_____	Time off
_____	Fun	_____	Toys
_____	Health	_____	Travel
_____	Honesty	_____	Winning

Mankind's greatest gift, also its greatest curse, is that we have free choice. We can make our choices built from love or from fear.

–Dr. Elizabeth Kublar-Ross

Look back on recent episodes. Make a list of your options. Include your "acting out" behavior as that puts it into the realm of choice versus "It just happened!"

EPISODE 1: _____

_____

_____

Option 1 _____

_____

_____

_____

Option 2 _____

_____

_____

_____

Option 3 _____

_____

_____

_____

Option 4 _____

_____

_____

_____

Option 5 _____

_____

Option 6 _____

_____

_____

Option 7 _____

_____

_____

Option 8 _____

_____

_____

Option 9 _____

_____

_____

Option 10 _____

_____

_____

EPISODE 2: _____

_____

_____

Option 1 _____

_____

_____

_____

Option 2 _____

_____

_____

_____

Option 3 _____

_____

_____

_____

Option 4 _____

_____

_____

_____

Option 5 _____

_____

_____

_____

Option 6 _____

_____

_____

_____

Option 7 _____

_____

_____

_____

Option 8 _____

_____

_____

_____

Option 9 _____

_____

_____

_____

Option 10 _____

_____

_____

_____

EPISODE 3: _____

_____

_____

Option 1 _____

_____

_____

_____

Option 2 _____

_____

_____

_____

Option 3 _____

_____

_____

_____

Option 4 _____

_____

_____

_____

Option 5 _____

_____

_____

_____

Option 6 _____

_____

_____

_____

Option 7 _____

_____

_____

_____

Option 8 _____

_____

_____

_____

Option 9 _____

_____

_____

_____

Option 10 _____

_____

_____

_____

<u>EPISODE 4</u>: _____

_____

_____

Option 1 _____

_____

_____

Option 2 _____

_____

_____

Option 3 _____

_____

_____

Option 4 _____

_____

_____

Option 5 _____

_____

_____

Option 6 _____

_____

_____

_____

Option 7 _____

_____

_____

_____

Option 8 _____

_____

_____

_____

Option 9 _____

_____

_____

_____

Option 10 _____

_____

_____

_____

EPISODE 5: _____

_____

_____

Option 1 _____

_____

_____

_____

Option 2 _____

_____

_____

_____

Option 3 _____

_____

_____

_____

Option 4 _____

_____

_____

_____

Option 5 _____

_____

_____

_____

Option 6 _____

_____

_____

_____

Option 7 _____

_____

_____

_____

Option 8 _____

_____

_____

_____

Option 9 _____

_____

_____

_____

Option 10 _____

_____

_____

_____

Mistakes are a part of being human. Appreciate your mistakes for what they are: precious life lessons that can only be learned the hard way. Unless it's a fatal mistake, which, at least, others can learn from.

−AL FRANKEN, *Oh, the Things I Know*

The indispensable first step to getting the things you want out of life is this: decide what you want.

−BEN STEIN

C is for Consequences

When you're "acting out," you are probably not thinking of the consequences of your behavior. And yet consequences always follow choices. Realizing what might happen as a result of your behavior can change the behaviors you choose. With each option you have listed, either in your mind or on a piece of paper, take a look at what the consequences might be. You might ask yourself, "If I choose this option what is the best that could happen, what is the worst that could happen, and what is most likely to happen?" Many people in 12-step groups will tell you to live in the present moment; to focus on the now rather than the past or the present. This can be sound advice in many instances. However, when you're in the process of acting out – thinking ahead to the consequences can help curb your behavior.

- **Art's Possible Consequences:**

    1. Taking out the trash and helping the kids with their homework demonstrates to his wife and children that he's trying to rebuild connection with them. However, there may be some resentment on his part if he doesn't get a chance to chill when he gets home.

    2. Ignoring his wife and kids increases their sense of

separation, causes feelings of hurt and rejection, and brings the couple closer to divorce.

3. Leaving the house angry and getting drunk most likely causes additional violence and lands him in jail for a long time.

4. Talking with his wife and agreeing to help while setting boundaries creates a growth experience for the whole family. He takes care of himself and still shows his wife and children that he cares about them and wants to contribute to the needs of the family.

• **Sue's Possible Consequences**

1. Seeing Mary always means getting drunk with her.

2. Stopping at a liquor store and buying booze leads to the same result – getting drunk. Getting drunk and choosing relapse brings Sue closer to serious illness and death.

3. Continuing on with her errands, Sue realizes that she does have the strength to get past cravings and keep herself on track for the rest of the day.

4. Sue finds the love and support she needs at AA meetings. There she has a sense of belonging and finds healing.

5. Calling her sponsor is almost as good as going to a meeting and doesn't take as much time. Tootsie, her sponsor, is good at helping her work through the problem issues and choosing personal responsibility.

6. Going home and taking care of herself replenishes her physical and emotional energy. She can plan another time to do the errands. Self care is not self-ish. After taking care of herself at home, she can call her sponsor

and work on some of her issues.

- **Pat's Possible Consequences**

  1. Booking his Las Vegas trip brings Pat closer to losing his house and increasing his debt.

  2. Calling his credit counselor and working on a spending plan helps Pat get out of debt, save his house, and curtail future spending.

  3. Going to the gym releases Pat's anxiety, reduces his urge to gamble, and clears his head to make better decisions.

  4. Going online to shop just exacerbates Pat's problem and leads to more spending and the loss of his house.

- **Glenda's** Possible Consequences

  1. Buying and eating binge food leads to purging and feelings of worthlessness, helplessness and self-hatred.

  2. Making herself a healthy dinner from what she has in her kitchen satisfies her hunger. She feels confident and in control of herself and her life.

  3. Going to bed hungry causes Glenda to feel deprived and ravenous in the morning, and yet she may also feel able to control her cravings.

  4. Eating something healthy and then figuring out a food plan deals with both the present and the future in a positive way.

  5. By calling her sponsor, Glenda gets support and help in deciding what she really wants without self-medicating with food.

• **Sylvia's Possible Consequences**

1. Falling in a heap means that Sylvia is mortified by the attention she attracts and the feelings of ridiculousness that engulf her.

2. Running away and leaving the store reinforces her fearful behavior and puts her at risk for getting in an accident.

3. Using breath work and positive self-talk, Sylvia realizes her feelings are temporary and fluid. She discovers that a little discomfort need not cause panic.

4. Continuing to shop without using her recovery tools is, at best, a white knuckle affair, creating misery throughout her shopping and causing her anxiety for future shopping trips.

5. Finding a place to sit down and pull herself together gets rid of the spotlight effect and she utilizes her tools more effectively.

• **Jack's Possible Consequences**

1. Cruising and finding a score puts Jack at risk for mugging, venereal disease, and divorce.

2. By going home to his wife, Jack begins rebuilding the trust he's lost through his "sexual acting out" behavior.

3. Jack's sponsor most likely creates a verbal contract with him to go immediately home. Jack then checks in with his sponsor when he gets home, creating a book-end like structure for Jack.

4. Pulling out his emergency kit helps Jack focus on what's really important to him. He reads his

meditation, looks at pictures of his kids, reads his list of reasons to not act out, and says his affirmations. This helps break the trance that leads to addictive behavior.

5. Stopping at a bar and having a drink is another step towards acting out sexually. Alcohol impairs the judgment center of the brain so he is more likely to get in trouble.

I want to be a jerk like the rest of my friends, and have fun, and not care about the consequences, but I can't just now.

–LEONARDO DICAPRIO

What are the consequences you have experienced due to your addictive/compulsive behaviors? Take each behavior and make a list of the consequences of that behavior. Take time to be thorough and look at every aspect of your life: physical, emotional, mental, spiritual, home and family, financial, work, social, jail/prison, community, school, goals, other.

Behavior _____

Consequences:

Physical _____

Emotional _____

Mental _____

Spiritual _____

Relation _____

Home/family _____

Financial _____

Work _____

Social _____

Jail/prison _____

Community _____

School _____

Goals _____

Other _____

Behavior _____

Consequences:

Physical _____

Emotional _____

Mental _____

Spiritual _____

Relation _____

Home/family _____

Financial _____

Work _____

Social _____

Jail/prison _____

Community _____

School _____

Goals _____

Other _____

_____

_____

_____

_____

_____

_____

Behavior _____

Consequences:

Physical _____

Emotional _____

Mental _____

Spiritual _____

Relation _____

Home/family_____

Financial _____

Work _____

Social _____

Jail/prison _____

Community _____

School _____

Goals _____

Other _____

_____

_____

_____ _____

_____

_____

_____

Behavior _____

Consequences:

Physical _____

Emotional _____

Mental _____

Spiritual _____

Relation _____

Home/family_____

Financial _____

Work _____

Social _____

Jail/prison _____

Community _____

School _____

Goals _____

Other _____

_____

_____

_____ _____

_____

_____

_____

What are the likely consequences if you continue your "acting out" behaviors?

Behavior _____

Consequences:

Physical _____

Emotional _____

Mental _____

Spiritual _____

Relation _____

Home/family _____

Financial _____

Work _____

Social _____

Jail/prison _____

Community _____

School _____

Goals _____

Other _____

_____

_____

_____

Behavior _____

Consequences:

Physical _____

Emotional _____

Mental _____

Spiritual _____

Relation _____

Home/family_____

Financial _____

Work _____

Social _____

Jail/prison _____

Community _____

School _____

Goals _____

Other _____

_____

_____

_____ _____

_____

_____

_____

Behavior _____

Consequences:

Physical _____

Emotional _____

Mental _____

Spiritual _____

Relation _____

Home/family_____

Financial _____

Work _____

Social _____

Jail/prison _____

Community _____

School _____

Goals _____

Other _____

_____

_____

_____

_____

_____

_____

Behavior _____

Consequences:

Physical _____

Emotional _____

Mental _____

Spiritual _____

Relation _____

Home/family_____

Financial _____

Work _____

Social _____

Jail/prison _____

Community _____

School _____

Goals _____

Other _____

_____

_____

_____

_____

_____

_____

Of the seven deadly sins, anger is possibly the most fun. To lick your wounds, to smack your lips over grievances long past, to roll over your tongue the prospect of bitter confrontations still to come, to savor to the last toothsome morsel both the pain you are given and the pain you are giving back — in many ways it is a feast fit for a king. The chief drawback is that what you are wolfing down is yourself. The skeleton at the feast is you.

—FREDERICK BUECHNER

U is for Use Positive Self-Talk

Building positive self-talk is one of the more powerful tools you can use to manage your life and regain control over your behavior. What you create in your mind becomes your reality. Whatever you direct your attention to expands. Intention is a catalyst for creation. Such small statements have a large impact. Everything in the material world began with a thought. Your perceptions shape what you believe. Your beliefs create your thoughts. Your thoughts affect what you feel. Your feelings influence your behavior.

The world is an interesting place. People create such pain and misery for themselves or each other: focusing on lack; what's wrong; what's missing; what hurts; who's being mean to them; not enough money; not enough time; not enough clothes; not enough things; focusing on the negative.

Your mandate is to use your mind with purpose; to make choices with awareness. Are your thoughts and beliefs in alignment with your desires and intentions? If not, what do you need to change so there is congruence within you?

When you realize the great power you have to create a happy and harmonious life, full of purpose and fulfillment, merely by wisely choosing positive thoughts, you may find yourself living in a different world, a world of transformation and wonder.

Affirmations, positive statements, are the simplest and easiest way to change self-talk. The key to using affirmations is to state your desire, in the present tense, as if it's already true. Avoid negatives. Your sub-conscious does not recognize negatives. So instead of saying, "I won't smoke anymore" use the phrase, "I am now free from smoking."

In the beginning, it is important to build affirmations that relate to the stinking thinking that creates your problem behavior. Through continued use of this tool you recreate the thoughts in your head and are able to change your belief system. Positive and healthy thinking then become your reality.

- **Art's Positive Self-Talk**

    1. I am able to recognize the needs of my wife and children.

    2. I am a strong and reliable husband and father.

    3. I give myself permission to take care of my own needs while responding to the needs of others.

    4. I deal with discomfort in a positive way.

    5. I can be a man's man and still be loving and giving

- **Sue's Positive Self-Talk**

    1. For me, self-care is not self-ish.

    2. I make decisions that are healthy for my body and my mind.

    3. I allow myself to feel pain without the need to medicate.

    4. Today I use the tools for my recovery.

5. Today I commit to recovery and all of the benefits that come with it.

- **Pat's Positive Self-Talk**

    1. I am enough. I have enough. I do enough.

    2. I commit to making choices that are best for me in the long run.

    3. I am open and willing to receive all of the abundance the universe has to offer me.

    4. I let go of my need for risk and stimulation.

    5. I am peaceful, happy and abundant.

- **Glenda's Positive Self-Talk**

    1. I love my body just as it is.

    2. I know what to do to take care of myself.

    3. I love myself. I approve of myself. I appreciate myself.

    4. I can and do change the rules I live by.

    5. I control my thoughts, beliefs, feelings and actions.

- **Sylvia's Positive Self-Talk**

    1. I deal with discomfort in a positive way.

    2. I am surrounded by love and concern.

    3. I am in charge of my body and the way it responds to the environment.

    4. Life is an adventure and I am ready for it.

    5. I dare to risk embarrassment or discomfort to achieve the life I want.

- **Jack's Positive Self-Talk**

  1. I value myself and I value others.

  2. I love and accept myself with all my flaws and defects.

  3. I am free of my addiction to sex and sexual stimulation.

  4. I go with the flow.

  5. I understand and acknowledge my needs and work to have my needs met in a healthy way.

It is not the critic who counts, not the man who points out how the strong man stumbled, or where the doer of deeds could have done better. The credit belongs to the man who is actually in the arena, whose face is marred by dust and sweat and blood; who strives valiantly; who errs and comes short again and again, who knows the great enthusiasms, the great devotions, and spends himself in a worthy cause; who at best, knows the triumph of high achievement; and who, at the worst, if he fails, at least fails while daring greatly, so that his place shall never be with those cold and timid souls who know neither victory nor defeat.

–THEODORE ROOSEVELT,
speech titled "Citizen in a Republic"
delivered at the Sorbonne, Paris, April 23, 1910

What affirmations will help you change? I have created some affirmations that might be helpful to you. But the most powerful affirmations are the ones you create and that pertain directly to you. Feel free to use those from the list or create your own.

Create your affirmations here:

_____

_____

_____

_____

_____

_____

_____

_____

_____

_____

_____

_____

_____

_____

_____

_____

_____

I invite you to say your affirmation, out loud and in your mind, to yourself at least three times a day. You might want to write them on post-it notes and paste them at various places around your home, at work, and on the dashboard of your car. Or write them on index cards and carry them with you in your pocket or in your purse. My husband and I have been sharing affirmations since 1995. We say three affirmations about ourselves out loud and then our partner affirms our statement. For instance, I say, "I love myself, I approve of myself, I appreciate myself." Larry responds, "Yes you do!" It is a powerful exercise that builds a sense of love and acceptance between the two of us. At first, it was difficult for me to come up with three affirmations. Now I pack several into one. My most important affirmation is one that has evolved over the years, building what I needed in my life. Here it is, "I am a wondrous and glorious, beautiful and intelligent, lovable and loving, bold, strong, positive and creative woman who deserves to be happy. Today I take steps to create happiness in my life and the lives of those around me."

The trick is in what one emphasizes. We either make ourselves miserable, or we make ourselves happy. The amount of work is the same.

-CARLOS CASTANEDA

AFFIRMATIONS

All is well.

Humor is my ally.

I accept all aspects of myself.

I accept criticism with grace.

I accept my family and still remain my own person.

I acknowledge my inherent worth and dignity.

I allow my inner light to shine for others to see.

I allow myself to be childlike in wonder, awe and trust.

I am a fair-minded person.

I am a worthwhile person.

I am able to deal with problems in an effective way.

I am able to laugh at myself.

I am able to learn from others.

I am able to see other's points of view

I am able to see the positive in others.

I am abundant

I am an instrument of peace.

I am at peace with myself and with others.

I am aware of the beauty around me.

I am beautiful, inside and out.

I am calm, peaceful and loving.

I am capable of being by myself and being okay with it.

I am capable of dealing with my emotions and feelings.

I am changing for the better.

I am compassionate with myself.

I am complete within myself.

I am confident without arrogance.

I am connected with myself, others, God and nature.

I am considerate of others rights.

I am fair.

I am flexible.

I am free of my addiction to _____.

I am generous.

I am gentle and kind.

I am gentle and non-threatening.

I am gentle with myself.

I am gentle with others.

I am grateful for all of the gifts I have been given.

I am happy and at peace.

I am healthy in body, mind and spirit.

I am imperfect and worthwhile.

I am independent and free.

I am intelligent.

I am kind and considerate.

I am living a life of balance.

I am lovable.

I am loved.

I am my own person.

I am open to the feelings of others.

I am open to the thoughts and beliefs of others.

I am open-minded.

I am patient with my recovery.

I am patient with myself and others.

I am peaceful.

I am positive and creative.

I am resourceful.

I am responsible for my behavior.

I am responsible for my emotions and feelings.

I am responsible for my feelings, thoughts and actions.

I am responsible for my happiness.

I am sensitive.

I am truthful and kind.

I am truthful.

I am working toward my goals.

I am worthy and valuable.

I am worthy even though I feel unsure or uncertain.

I anticipate good things happening to me

I believe in myself.

I can and do let go of pride.

I can change the rules I live by.

I can deal with embarrassment in good humor.

I can deal with rejection.

I can share the deepest parts of myself with trustworthy people.

I choose healthy thoughts and emotions.

I choose to be happy.

I choose to take care of myself appropriately.

I commit to making life less difficult for myself and those around me.

I commit to my personal growth and discovery

I control my thoughts, beliefs, feelings and actions.

I control only myself.

I create my own happiness.

I create the life that I want.

I dare to dream.

I dare to grow.

I dare to risk embarrassment or discomfort to achieve my goals.

I dare to try something new in order to grow.

I deal with discomfort in a positive way.

I deflect all personal attacks.

I deserve love.

I deserve to be happy and today I make choices that create happiness in my life

I deserve to be happy.

I determine my destiny.

I embrace diversity.

I enjoy solitude.

I express my anger openly and honestly in an appropriate manner.

I express myself directly.

I face my fears with courage.

I face the truth with a positive attitude.

I feel powerful and positive.

I follow my dreams.

I forgive myself and others.

I forgive past and present hurts.

I give and receive happily.

I give and receive respect.

I give openly and honestly, without expecting something in return.

I go with the flow.

I have a positive attitude.

I have many choices in any situation.

I have peace in my heart.

I have positive visions of the future.

I hear others without the need to protect myself.

I hear the pain, fear, sorrow and frustration of another without taking it on myself.

I help others as well as myself.

I honor the food I eat.

I know the truth.

I know what to do to take care of myself.

I laugh freely.

I let go of anger.

I let go of being right, or needing to be right.

I let go of fear and distrust.

I let go of my defensiveness.

I let go of resentment.

I let go of shame.

I let go of stereotypes.

I let go of worry.

I listen beyond the spoken word.

I listen to my inner voice with confidence.

I listen with an open mind.

I listen with compassion.

I listen without getting defensive.

I live consciously.

I live in the here and now.

I live in the present moment.

I look at my past free of shame.

I look forward to this day.

I love me and every part of me.

I love my inner child.

I love myself. I approve of myself. I appreciate myself.

I make decisions that are healthy for my mind, body and spirit.

I make decisions with confidence and clarity.

I make time for myself.

I make time for my family and friends.

I open myself to all of the goodness in the universe.

I open myself to new friends.

I open myself to the viewpoint of others.

I own my part in past hurts.

I pay attention to details and clear up loose ends.

I pay attention to my needs.

I perceive myself as worthwhile.

I relax and trust that all is well.

I remember the past and heal from it.

I respect my body.

I respect myself.

I respect myself and others.

I respect others.

I see the fear behind anger directed towards me.

I see the hurt behind anger directed towards me.

I seek out the unknown, confident in myself.

I take action.

I take care of myself.

I take my actions seriously.

I treasure my solitude.

I treat my children with respect.

I treat my spouse with respect.

I trust God, believe in myself, dare to dream and take action.

I trust God.

I trust myself to handle anything that comes my way in a healthy manner.

I trust my spouse.

I trust others.

I trust that what happens is always for the best.

I understand and acknowledge my needs.

I understand my needs and work towards getting them met in an appropriate way.

I use invitation versus confrontation.

I use my mind and thoughts to create the life I want.

I use *Stop – Breathe – Focus*.

I use the Universal Principles and Laws.

I value all living things.

I value all things on earth.

I value life.

I value my own and other people's thoughts, feelings and beliefs.

I value myself and I value others.

I value people who are different than myself.

I view myself and my situation with love and compassion.

I welcome company.

I work through whatever situation I am in appropriately.

Life is an adventure.

Love is a verb.

My body and my mind are quiet and content.

My feelings are constantly changing.

My home is a place of laughter and love.

My mind is quiet and I enjoy solitude.

My mistakes are opportunities for growth.

My need for love is fulfilled.

My needs will be met, by others, by myself, by God.

My problem beliefs are changing for the better.

Today I face the truth without shame.

Today I fill my life with harmony.

Today I focus on the solution instead of the problem.

Today I make healthy choices.

Today I reframe my "stinking thinking."

Today I remain balanced and objective.

Today I take steps to create happiness in my life and the lives of those around me.

Today I treat others the way I would like to be treated.

Today I use my tools for recovery.

Today I work toward partnership versus competition.

Uncertainty is filled with limitless possibilities.

Yes!

Once you replace negative thoughts with positive ones, you'll start having positive results.

–WILLIE NELSON

S is for Self-Responsibility

Personal accountability is the source of personal power. Sometimes you blame others for the choices you make. "If only he hadn't left that candy out on the counter, I wouldn't have eaten it." "She made me so mad I couldn't control myself. I had to hit her." "If my girlfriend didn't leave me, I wouldn't have gotten drunk." "My boss is such a jerk. He fired me just because I came late to work a couple of times."

You are the only one responsible for your behavior. No one makes you do anything. You always have a choice; actually you have three choices in every situation. You may not like the consequences of some of the choices but the choices are there. Taking responsibility for your behavior is liberating and empowering. It removes you from being a victim and creates a mindset of power. It is important not to blame anyone for your behavior; not even yourself. Blame is a disempowering behavior that isn't fair to anyone, especially you. Blaming others leaves you feeling like a victim. Blaming yourself leads to self-loathing, non-productive guilt and shame. Dealing with situations honestly and accepting responsibility for your behavior leads to a life of integrity.

- **Art's Responsibility** – Art realizes that his wife and kids are merely expressing their needs and the way he responds to their needs, and his own, determines the health of their relationships. He used to deny the scope of his violence and how it affected his family.

• **Sue's Responsibility** – Sue realizes she has been minimizing the effects of her drinking on the family. She also realizes she has been blaming her responsibilities as a wife and mother for her drinking and for feeling cheated out of having fun. Sue understands that she can create a life of fun, joy peace and happiness by staying sober. It is up to her.

• **Pat's Responsibility** – Pat kept saying to himself, "If I don't have fun now or buy the things that I want now, I'll never have them." He understands this is stinking thinking. By controlling his spending and developing a financial plan he can provide all that he needs in the form of recreation and self gratification in a healthy manner. He is determined to live within his means.

• **Glenda's Responsibility** – Glenda has always blamed her mother for teaching her to self-medicate her sadness and unworthiness with food. Glenda admits that her own choices and decisions determine what, when and how much she eats. She is responsible for breaking this cycle of behavior by loving herself and making food choices based on love rather than fear or loathing.

• **Sylvia's Responsibility** – Sylvia has been afraid to live life since her mother died. Sylvia's insight that the attention she draws to herself during her panic attacks are a means of feeling cared about, even if it is by strangers or coworkers. Sylvia realizes the answers are within herself.

• **Jack's Responsibility** – Jack finally understands that anger, frustration and shame drive his sexually addictive behavior. Rather than blaming the women who wear short skirts or have on a lot of makeup, he decides to be fully responsible. He used to always say, "Boys will be boys!" or "I'm just full of testosterone!" or "If I'm going to have an addiction, this is the one I want!" Now Jack realizes that he is in charge of the way he behaves and that no one is responsible for the decisions he makes but him.

The three principle barriers to self-responsibility are blaming, denying and minimizing. Blaming is pointing the finger at someone else, or even yourself. Minimizing is making an act seem smaller than it actually was. Example: "She bruises easily. If I just breathe on her the wrong way she gets a bruise." Denying is about refusing to admit what you did (to yourself or others). Example: "It wasn't me." "I didn't do that."

When you come to the end of all the light you know, and it's time to step into the darkness of the unknown, faith is knowing that one of two things shall happen: Either you will be given something solid to stand on or you will be taught to fly.

—EDWARD TELLER

DENIAL

What are some examples of your use of denial?

Situation: _____

_____

Ways you used denial _____

_____

_____

Situation: _____

_____

Ways you used denial _____

_____

_____

Situation: _____

_____

Ways you used denial _____

_____

_____

Situation: _____

_____

Ways you used denial _____

_____

_____

Situation: _____

_____

Ways you used denial _____

_____

_____

Situation: _____

_____

Ways you used denial _____

_____

_____

Notes: _____

_____

_____

_____

_____

_____

_____

_____

_____

_____

_____

_____

_____

_____

_____

_____

MINIMIZATION

What are some examples of your use of Minimization?

Situation: _____

_____

Ways you used denial _____

_____

_____

Situation: _____

_____

Ways you used denial _____

_____

_____

Situation: _____

_____

Ways you used denial _____

_____

_____

Situation: _____

_____

Ways you used denial _____

_____

_____

Situation: _____

_____

Ways you used denial _____

_____

_____

Situation: _____

_____

Ways you used denial _____

_____

_____

Notes: _____

_____

_____

_____

_____

_____

_____

_____

_____

_____

_____

_____

_____

_____

_____

BLAME

What are ways you blamed, self or others?

Situation: _____

_____

Ways you used denial _____

_____

_____

Situation: _____

_____

Ways you used denial _____

_____

_____

Situation: _____

_____

Ways you used denial _____

_____

_____

Situation: _____

_____

Ways you used denial _____

_____

_____

Situation: _____

_____

Ways you used denial _____

_____

_____

Situation: _____

_____

Ways you used denial _____

_____

_____

Notes: _____

_____

_____

_____

_____

_____

_____

_____

_____

_____

_____

_____

Ultimately self-responsibility is about being fully honest and accountable to yourself and others for your behavior, attitudes, beliefs, feelings and every aspect of yourself and your actions.

Now that you've acknowledged times when you minimized, denied and blamed, it's important that you look at times when you were able to be honest and accountable, even in difficult situations; with predictable consequences. Remember that personal responsibility is different than blaming oneself. Self-responsibility is about owning behavior and consequences rather than beating yourself up. Please list some situations where you were able to own your behavior.

Situation: _____

_____

Ways you were honest and accountable: _____

_____

_____

_____

Situation: _____

_____

Ways you were honest and accountable: _____

_____

_____

_____

Situation: _____

_____

Ways you were honest and accountable: _____

_____

_____

_____

Situation: _____

_____

Ways you were honest and accountable: _____

_____

_____

_____

Situation: _____

_____

Ways you were honest and accountable: _____

_____

_____

_____

RESPONSE-ABILITY

Finally, I invite you to: Use your power to respond to life in a manner which creates health and happiness for you and others; Allow your inherent worth and dignity to guide your way; manifest your inner goodness as you are meant to do; focus on gratitude for the positive aspects of your life; look for the lessons in every challenge you face; Find humor in difficult situations; employ positive and creative thoughts, feelings, beliefs and behaviors; know and utilize your strengths; have faith; shine your inner light upon the world.

The best years of your life are the ones in which you decide your problems are your own. You do not blame them on your mother, the ecology, or the president. You realize that you control your own destiny.

—ALBERT ELLIS

Stop – Breathe – Focus

So, when faced with behaviors and situations that create problems for you, use the best tool you have.
Stop – Breathe – Focus!

Stop: Say "stop" to yourself as you put your hand to your heart.

Breathe: Breathe in through your nose, out through your mouth. Breathe in half as long as you breathe out. In – four – out eight. In – three – out – six. In – two – out – four. Take a few in and out breathes if your chest feels like it's made of concrete.

Focus: Bring your attention to your body, heart, mind and spirit.

F – Feelings and Thoughts: Notice how you're feeling physically, emotionally, mentally and spiritually. Use descriptive words. Avoid good, bad, okay, fine or any other judgmental word. Also notice the self-talk that is going on in your head, particularly how the self-talk relates to your feelings and behavior.

O – Options: Identify as many options as possible. Remember there are always at least three options for any given situation. Even animals have three options; to flee, to fight, and to freeze.

C – Consequences: What will happen if you make certain choices? What's the best that will happen? What's the worst that will happen? What's most likely to happen?

U – Use Positive Self-Talk: Build positive self-talk to counter the negative self-talk. Say affirmations often.

S – Self Responsibility: You're responsible for your behavior. Choose options that are healthy for you! Blame, either toward another person or you, is a destructive behavior that can lead to feelings of anger, powerlessness and victimization.

The Choice is Yours!